"The importance of Helfta monastery in medieval religious culture is well established, as is the role of Gertrud the Great. Barratt's translation of Gertrud's *Herald*, which makes this profoundly significant text accessible in a polished and reliable rendition, is now complete with the publication of Book 5, along with related material from Mechtild of Hackeborn. Book 5 deals with the terminal illnesses, deaths, and afterlives of nuns and others connected with Helfta, and it shows how posthumous purgation and the intercession of the living were viewed in a late medieval setting. As Barratt points out, this final book also gives rich depiction of the monastic community. This book is the capstone to a project of the utmost significance for the study of medieval religious culture."

    —Richard Kieckhefer
    Northwestern University

"With this book, Alexandra Barratt completes her translation of all five parts of *Herald of God's Loving-Kindness* and therefore significantly contributes to Gertrudian studies. Her inclusion of parts six and seven of *The Book of Special Grace,* associated with Mecthild of Hackeborn, provides an invaluable tool for continuing scholarship on the thirteenth-century Helfta community."

    —Ella Johnson, author of *This Is My Body: Eucharistic Theology and*
    Anthropology in the Writings of Gertrude the Great of Helfta

D1563027

CISTERCIAN FATHERS SERIES: NUMBER EIGHTY-SIX

GERTRUD THE GREAT OF HELFTA

THE HERALD OF GOD'S LOVING-KINDNESS

BOOK FIVE

and

MECHTILD OF HACKEBORN

THE BOOK OF SPECIAL GRACE

PARTS SIX AND SEVEN

Translated and Introduced by Alexandra Barratt

Cistercian Publications
www.cistercianpublications.org

LITURGICAL PRESS
Collegeville, Minnesota
www.litpress.org

A Cistercian Publications title published by Liturgical Press

Cistercian Publications
Editorial Offices
161 Grosvenor Street
Athens, Ohio 45701
www.cistercianpublications.org

1   2   3   4   5   6   7   8   9

Library of Congress Cataloging-in-Publication Data

Names: Barratt, Alexandra, translator. | Gertrude, the Great, Saint, 1256-1302. Legatus divinae pietatis. Book 5. English | Mechthild, of Hackeborn, 1241 or 1242-1299? Liber specialis gratiae. Book 6-7. English

Title: Gertrud the Great of Helfta, The herald of God's loving-kindness, book five and Mechtild of Hackeborn, The book of special grace, parts six and seven / translated and introduced by Alexandra Barratt.

Other titles: The herald of God's loving-kindness, book five

Description: Collegeville, Minnesota : Cistercian Publications, Liturgical Press 2020. | Series: Cistercian fathers ; number eighty-six | Summary: "Book 5 details the sickness, deaths, and afterlife fates of various Helfta nuns, novices, and lay brothers, as witnessed by Gertrud in her visions. It also describes Gertrud's preparations for her own death and her predictive visions of her ultimate glorification in heaven"— Provided by publisher.

Identifiers: LCCN 2020011235 (print) | LCCN 2020011236 (ebook) | ISBN 9780879071868 (paperback) | ISBN 9780879075866 (epub) | ISBN 9780879075866 (mobi) | ISBN 9780879075866 (pdf)

Subjects: LCSH: Gertrude, the Great, Saint, 1256-1302. | Mechthild, of Hackeborn, 1241 or 1242-1299? | Mysticism—Germany—History—Middle Ages, 600-1500—Sources. | Christian women saints—Germany—Death. | Women mystics—Germany—Death. | Private revelations.

Classification: LCC BV5091.A1 G4713 2020 (print) | LCC BV5091.A1 (ebook) | DDC 248.2/2—dc23

LC record available at https://lccn.loc.gov/2020011235

LC ebook record available at https://lccn.loc.gov/2020011236

CONTENTS

ABBREVIATIONS

CF	Cistercian Fathers series
LDP	Gertrude the Great of Helfta, *The Herald of God's Loving-Kindness*
SBOp	Sancti Bernardi Opera
SC	Bernard of Clairvaux, Sermons on the Song of Songs
SCh	Sources chrétiennes
Special Grace	Mechtild of Hackeborn, *Liber Specialis Gratiae*

INTRODUCTION

Readers who have come as far as the fifth and final book of *The Herald of God's Loving-Kindness* will no doubt already know the essential facts about Gertrud the Great (1256–1302), to whose name this text is attached. She was a German nun at the monastery of Helfta, founded in 1229 and situated in what is today Saxony-Anhalt, Germany.[1] Under Gertrud of Hackeborn, who had become abbess at the age of nineteen in 1251, three of Helfta's members wrote mystical treatises in the late thirteenth century: Mechtild of Hackeborn, author of *The Book of Special Grace*;[2] Gertrud (distinct from the abbess), source of *The Herald of God's Loving-Kindness,* of which she wrote Book 2 herself, while a close confidante, now known as "Sister N.,"[3] compiled the other four books; and Mechtild

---

1. On Helfta and its history, see the documents reprinted in *Revelationes Gertrudianae ac Mechtildianae* II, ed. L. Paquelin (Paris: Oudin, 1877), 714–28; Alexandra Barratt, trans. and annot., *Gertrud the Great of Helfta: The Herald of God's Loving-Kindness: Books One and Two*, CF 35 (Kalamazoo, MI: Cistercian Publications, 1991), 7–8; Alexandra Barratt and Debra L. Stoudt, "Gertrude the Great of Helfta," in *Medieval Holy Women in the Christian Tradition c. 1000–c. 1500,* ed. Alastair Minnis and Rosalynn Voaden (Turnhout: Brepols, 2010), 454–55; Josef Hochenauer, *Kloster Helfta: Raum schaffen für das Licht* (Bamberg: St Otto, 1999).

2. There is now an English translation of much of this lengthy treatise: *Mechtild of Hackeborn and the Nuns of Helfta: The Book of Special Grace*, Barbara Newman, intro. and trans. (Mahwah, NJ: Paulist, 2017). The translation is selective, and the material has been somewhat rearranged. Translations here from *The Book of Special Grace* are my own.

3. See Balázs J. Nemes, "Text Production and Authorship: Gertrude of Helfta's *Legatus divinae pietatis*," in Elizabeth Andersen, Henrike Lähnemann, and Anne Simon, eds., *A Companion to Mysticism and Devotion in Northern Germany in the Late Middle Ages* (Leiden and Boston: Brill, 2014), 116–20; and Almuth Märker and Balázs J. Nemes, *"Hunc tercium conscripsi cum maximo labore*

of Magdebourg, a Beguine, who composed Book 7 of her vernacular treatise *The Flowing Light of the Godhead* at Helfta, where she found refuge late in life. The abbess and both Mechtilds figure prominently in Book 5.

Gertrud's earthly life was externally uneventful but internally intense. She was born on the feast of the Epiphany in 1256 and was offered to Helfta by her family at the age of four (child oblation was still practised in Benedictine houses, even though the Cistercians had abandoned the practice): we can only imagine how traumatic it must have been for the future saint to be wrenched from her parents at such a young age, however kind the abbess who received her. A few years before, in 1259, Helfta had moved from its site in Rodardsdorf to new and better buildings in Eisleben, and no doubt it was raising its profile and increasing its intake. In the monastery the young Gertrud received an excellent medieval education in the *trivium* (Latin grammar, rhetoric, and dialectic) and possibly in the *quadrivium* (arithmetic, music, geometry, and astronomy): the abbess was a firm believer in the importance of such learning for the proper understanding of Scripture and, consequently, for the promotion of the religious life, as we learn from *Special Grace* VI.1. Originally indifferent to the vocation foisted upon her, in 1281 at the age of twenty-five Gertrud underwent a conversion and was thenceforward favored with numerous visions and mystical experiences, in which the divine heart of Jesus played a large part. Although frequently confused with the abbess of the same name, she never held conventual office (apart from acting as deputy chantress, as emerges in V.1.24).[4] Rather, she was renowned for her teaching, her composition

---

occultandi: Schwester N von Helfta und ihre 'Sonderausgabe' des 'Legatus divinae pietatis' Gertruds von Helfta in der Leipziger Handschrift Ms 827," in *Beiträge zur Geschichte der deutschen Sprache und Literatur* 137 (2015): 248–96.

4. References to Book 5 of *The Herald* are to the present translation; references to Books 1 and 2 are to Alexandra Barratt, trans., *The Herald: Books One and Two*, CF35 (Kalamazoo, MI: Cistercian Publications, 1991); references to Book 3 to Alexandra Barratt, trans., *Gertrud the Great of Helfta: The Herald of God's Loving-Kindness: Book Three*, CF 63 (Kalamazoo, MI: Cistercian Publications, 1999); and references to Book 4 to Alexandra Barratt, trans., *Gertrud the Great*

of prayers and spiritual florilegia,[5] and her role as spiritual advisor and intermediary with the divine, which is central to much of Book 5. After many years of sickness she died in her mid-forties in 1301 or 1302.[6]

Structure of Book 5

Book 5 falls into two parts. The first twenty-two chapters present a series of exemplary accounts of the sickness, death, penitential sufferings, and eventual glorification of various people associated with the monastery of Helfta. Anyone who thinks this sounds like an unpromising subject is in for a surprise, for we probably learn more about Helfta as a community from this book alone than from the other four books of *The Herald* combined. The monastery emerges not as a homogeneous women's house, but as a diverse community made up of both men and women, religious and lay.

This section opens with ten chapters concerned with twelve women and girls. In pride of place is the lengthy appreciation of the abbess Gertrud, by far the longest of any of these essays. The abbess, who was a deft facilitator and efficient administrator rather than a visionary herself, has been overshadowed in the eyes of posterity by her nuns, but it is clear from both V.1 and *Special Grace* VI that she was a remarkable woman who set high standards of scholarship and piety, and whose leadership provided a sympathetic and sheltered environment in which the more mystically inclined could flourish. Second only in length to this eulogy of the abbess is that of

---

of Helfta: The Herald of God's Loving-Kindness: Book Four, CF 85 (Collegeville, MN: Cistercian Publications, 2018). References specifically to the Latin *Legatus* (LDP), the chapter and paragraph numbers of which are replicated in the translations, are to *Le Héraut*, ed. Pierre Doyère and others, SCh 25, 27, 225, and 331 (Paris: Éditions du Cerf, 1968–1986).

5. One possible example of her work in this genre has recently come to light in Leipzig, Universitätsbibliothek MS 827, beginning "Ducam eam in solitudinem."

6. Our meager information about Gertrud's life is derived from *The Herald* itself. See further Barratt, *The Herald: Books One and Two*, 9–12, and Barratt, *The Herald: Book Three*, 9–11.

her younger sister, Mechtild of Hackeborn (V.4), whose death and apotheosis are covered even more extensively in *Special Grace* VII (see further below).

Many of the other chapters concern novices and nuns of all ages (e.g. V.5), but we also find the Beguine Mechtild of Magdebourg (V.7), girls who had not yet taken any vows (V.2), and, possibly, a secular woman who had retired to the monastery (V.8). Known only as "M.B.," she is at fault because "she had sometimes taken pleasure in outward things, such as that her bed was draped with embroidered fabric with designs in gold, and the like" (V.8.1): no doubt the bed hangings were relics of her former life as a great lady. It is poignant that so many of these women are quite young: the infirmary at Helfta seems to have been a busy place.

None of these women is in any danger of damnation, and the controversial question of whether or not souls in hell can be saved by the prayers of the living is never confronted. But Gertrud, whose criticisms are channeled through the Lord in her visionary encounters, does have a sharp eye for the failings of her fellow community members. Even the abbess Gertrud is not entirely perfect: she herself admits somewhat cryptically that, with respect to the sense of touch, "I was slightly negligent there, although with good intentions and for the sake of peace" (V.1.29). (Perhaps she was given to hugging the little girls and novices.) Of the young girl E., our Lord himself implies that she is tainted by "less serious sins, such as taking pleasure in what is not strictly necessary and the like" (V.2.2). G., another young girl, though very devout, was "a little too attached to her own opinion" (V.3.2)—a typical teenager perhaps?—while the novices M. and E. suffered from "negligences" (V.5.3) and "certain stains" (V.5.2). More specifically, Dame Sophie the elder was not allowed to die "until she expiated by her sickness a single fault that she had committed, by offending against obedience in talking with an invalid more than was right" (V.6.1). Sisters G. and S. were sick in the infirmary at the same time: G. evinced "an unwillingness from time to time to make her confession," going so far as to pretend to be asleep when the priest visited (V.9.1), while in her sickness S. "used to enjoy certain things that she did not need, that is, gifts and consolation from her friends" (V.9.3), and manifested "attachment to earthly pleasure" (V.9.5).

None of these human weaknesses could possibly rank as more than venial sins, and their trivial nature seems disconcertingly at odds with the emphasis elsewhere in *The Herald* on God's loving-kindness. But Gertrud is insistent that these imperfections must all be purged before the soul can be truly acceptable to God and join the ranks of the inhabitants of heaven. So apart from Gertrud the abbess and the two Mechtilds, all these souls must endure various purgatorial pains that can be mitigated by their friends and fellow religious on earth, by offering prayers, special devotions, and the sacrifice of the Mass on their behalf, to hasten their triumphal entry into heaven. And such exertions are never wasted: if the soul for whom they are offered has no need of them, the benefits are passed on to others less fortunate.

Following the ten chapters on women are five on men, all lay-brothers. It is notable that they are treated as members of the community just as much as the nuns, but most are spiritually inferior to the women, and their souls are at greater risk. The kindly brother Seguinus alone escapes criticism and is rewarded for his loyalty to the community (V.11.1), but the soul of brother H. is punished, as he himself admits, for wilfulness—"when I did good, I used to take greater pleasure in carrying out my own "will than another's counsel" (V.12.3)—and a reluctance to forgive (V.12.5). The Lord himself explains that Gertrud's prayers for H. are less effective than they might be because "in the world he showed himself so obstinate and unyielding when it came to submitting his will to the will of those who for some reason were asking him for something that he himself did not want" (V.12.6). Brother John was the convent's steward, a role that posed many moral hazards (V.13.1), while brother Thomas, a humble laborer, had sometimes acted dishonestly (V.14.1). Brother F. is in the most parlous state: Gertrud sees his soul "in the form of a most disgusting toad, burning horribly within, and tormented by various sufferings for his faults" (V.15.1) because he "had failed to direct his understanding towards the things of God." More specifically, "without his superior's permission he had worked too hard to

acquire worldly goods and had also sometimes concealed his gains."
He also "had been insubordinate towards his superior." But even he
is not past praying for.

Chapters 16 and 17 describe the fates of various souls belonging
to relatives of members of the community. First we meet a soul in
serious danger of damnation. Gertrud sees him "as a toad, black as
coal, and contorted from the immensity of its[7] suffering. No torturer
was visible, but it was being inwardly tortured in each and every limb
by those sins that each limb had committed" (V.16.1). This obdurate
sinner had persisted in his sins for many years, and his soul is purified
only with the greatest difficulty. Then, in contrast, we meet a group
of souls, not just of relatives but also of the Lord's special friends,
who are released together into heaven.

The next two chapters concern a devotion, apparently peculiar
to Helfta, called "The Great Psalter." This seems to have been a
laborious recitation of the entire psalter interspersed with prayers,
combined with the offering of Masses and acts of almsgiving. Its
efficacy in releasing souls into heaven is illustrated by the story of
the soul of a knight who, of all those in Book 5, comes the closest
to damnation. Gertrud sees the soul "in the form of a huge beast that
seemed to have as many enormous horns as other beasts have hairs!
And this beast seemed to be poised above the mouth of hell, with
just a single branch under its left side supporting it. All the pain and
misery of hell, wafting towards him, tormented him with unbearable
and inconceivable torture" (V.19.1).

The knight had sinned in pride and has only escaped damnation
because "sometimes, though rarely, he had had some vestige of good
will while still alive." But he was not receiving "the least relief from
any of the church's prayers." Gertrud breaks this impasse by reciting the Great Psalter, after which the soul resumes human form as

---

7. Normally in this translation the soul (which in Latin is grammatically feminine) is given the gender of its possessor. However, when (as here) it manifests
itself in a non-human form, it is treated as neuter.

a little boy, though "still quite filthy" (V.19.2), and is able to access the common prayers of the church and, ultimately, to reach heaven.

Two short chapters develop the theme of the ways in which the living can benefit the dead, and this section concludes on a more sober and salutary note by demonstrating "the punishment of the disobedient and the detractors." The woman who exemplifies disobedience, following her own inclination rather than her superiors' commands in "sometimes preferring rigorous fasting, vigils, and the like" (V.22.1), is being punished, even though she repented before death. Another woman who "had listened to murmurs and detractions" is tortured grotesquely, even though she "acted without malice and had quite often repented" (V.22.3).

In the first half of Book 5, then, there is a clear downward movement from Gertrud, the ideal abbess and bride of Christ, to those who must suffer the heaviest purgatorial pains. As Gertrud herself remarks, "Alas! Lord, when once you used to show me souls' rewards, now you rather show purgation of sins." The Lord replied, "Then people were being attracted, but now they are being terrified, with difficulty, by torments!" (V.22.3).

The second half of Book 5 is introduced as follows: "Here we would like to append the consolations on the subject of her own death that God's most benign loving-kindness faithfully granted her" (V.23). The reader is no doubt by now expecting an account of Gertrud's own death similar to the accounts of the passing of others in chapters 1–15, but will wait in vain. All these earlier accounts follow the pattern of describing a last sickness, death-bed agonies, a passing fortified by the sacraments of the church, purification of the soul where necessary, and heavenly apotheosis. But only a visionary, of course, can witness most of this, and there is no visionary who can fill precisely the same role for Gertrud herself as she did for others. Instead, we have a sequence of ten chapters offering a detailed account of her growing desire for death (V.23.1 and V.25), the preparations that she makes (V.24), her anxiety that these may be wasted because death does not come as quickly as she expects (V.26), the performance of a particular devotion composed by herself to prepare for death (V.27), accounts of celestial consolations and divine promises (V.28, V.29), extended visionary dialogues with Christ and his mother (V.30, V.31), and, climactically, an anticipatory revelation of her death (V.32).

The final four chapters of Book 5 have perhaps attracted the most scholarly attention. They concern "the book," *The Herald of God's Loving-Kindness* itself, its divine authorization and endorsement. In V.33, Christ appears to Gertrud to vouch for its inerrancy and to emphasize the pleasure it gives him. In the following chapter, "Sister N." emerges from the shadows for the first and last time: "when the compiler [Sister N.] was about to receive communion, she was carrying this book hidden in her sleeve under her cloak to offer it to the Lord to his eternal praise without anyone's knowledge." She herself is no visionary, merely a humble amanuensis, so it is "another person" who reports seeing the Lord embrace her and promise that reading this book will be spiritually fruitful for all who approach it in humility, declaring, "if anyone comes to me with humble heart and wishes to read it for love of my love, truly I shall point out to that person [sitting] on my lap, as if with my own finger,[8] one by one, whatever is useful for them."

The penultimate chapter 35 is written in the first person, presumably by Sister N. herself rather than Gertrud. She offers Christ the book over which she has toiled for so long, describing it as "this nectar-sweet torrent of your generous loving-kindness that the powerful sweetness of your unsearchable divine nature has brought forth from the depths of your loving heart to inundate, water, fertilize, and bless the heart and soul of your chosen, to draw her and bind her indissolubly to yourself" (V.35.1).

She thanks the Lord in advance for all the graces that future readers will receive; she laments her own deficiencies as transmitter and begs forgiveness for any readers who fail to appreciate the value of the book. The final chapter emphasizes the book's incomplete nature—"very many, or rather, countless things have been omitted"—

---

8. Cf. IV.5.3, lines 21–24.

and the way in which it has been adapted, by divine help, to the limited capacities of the readers: "Leading his chosen one as if by the upward steps of images, [the Lord] conducted her to more hidden things, or rather to purer and more excellent draughts of wisdom, which the shadows of corporeal images could by no means bring to common knowledge" (V.36.1).

Reading this final suite of chapters within the context of the rest of Book 5, we can see that it is the text rather than Gertrud that is glorified and united with the divine in a final apotheosis.

The Theology of Book 5: Gertrud and Purgatory

Given Book 5's emphasis on death and its aftermath, we should briefly comment on Gertrud's beliefs on these subjects. They are contingent, and entirely orthodox for the time. By the late thirteenth century it was believed that after death, almost all those souls destined ultimately for salvation nonetheless had to undergo purification. In a very few cases, privileged and holy souls (such as the two Mechtilds in Book 5) are immediately glorified and admitted to the divine presence. Otherwise, purification is carried out through suffering, and/ or in a place of suffering. Some souls may be so deeply soiled that they cannot immediately access the common prayers of the church without special intercession; others, although Gertrud hardly ever mentions them, are damned if they die unrepentant in mortal sin. The exertions of the living can curtail the soul's ordeal by offering prayers and other devotions, alms, and Masses: praying for the dead was a well-established practice: "The theologians agreed that it might help to speed up or mitigate the process of purgation after death, or simply celebrate the passage of a saint to heaven . . . . In many cases, intercession was seen not just as helpful but as necessary to the salvation of a sinful soul."[9] Its effectiveness was partly dependent on the intercessors' own merits, as "only someone with special

9. Megan McLaughlin, *Consorting with Saints: Prayers for the Dead in Early Medieval France* (Ithaca and London: Cornell University Press, 1994), 212.

standing in the spiritual realm could hope to intervene effectively for imperilled souls."[10]

But the full development of such beliefs had not always held sway and would have seemed unfamiliar to Christians of an earlier era. Jacques Le Goff famously declared that although the church had believed for many centuries that prayers for the dead were beneficial, "the invention of purgatory," that is, belief in "an intermediary other world in which some of the dead were subjected to a trial that could be shortened by the prayers, by the spiritual aid, of the living," can be dated to "between 1150 and 1200 or so": in other words, only half a century before Gertrud was born.[11]

Even a cursory search on the Internet reveals that in some pious circles Gertrud is believed to have had a special care for souls in purgatory. Indeed, she is credited with a popular but completely in-authentic prayer that even today, in spite of the church's best efforts, many people believe will release a thousand souls from purgatory every time it is recited.[12] So it is instructive to examine what Gertrud does have to say about purgatory in her authentic writings. And the surprising answer is, not as much as one would expect.

Goff maintained that the Latin word *purgatorium* was introduced between 1170 and 1200,[13] so was a relative novelty when the Gertrud texts were being written down. A search for that word in its various forms in the five books of LDP throws up no more than five occurrences: two in Book 3 (III.18.6, lines 17 and 23), one in Book 4 (IV.35.9, line 6), and two in Book 5 (V.9.4, line 11, and V.10.1, line 22). Notably, there are no examples in Book 2, which Gertrud wrote "with her own hand." However, the idea of a state of purification that

10. McLaughlin, *Consorting with Saints,* 212.

11. Jacques Le Goff, trans. Arthur Goldhammer, *The Birth of Purgatory* (London: Scolar Press, 1984), 4.

12. Some optimists give figures of 50,000 or even 64,000. The story may derive, at several removes, from LDP III.9.

13. Le Goff, *Birth,* 149.

has to be endured after death is undoubtedly present in the Gertrud texts, but expressed by other words and phrases. For instance, souls need release "from suffering" (*a poenis*), and this phrase occurs at least another seven times, again in Books 3, 4, and 5, although *poena* can also mean trials and tribulations suffered in this life. Or souls are described as *purgand-* , "requiring to be purified," and the process itself as *purgatio*: both these terms are even more common. This strongly suggests that Gertrud's concept of purgatory was primarily of a state, or condition, of the soul, rather than a place of punishment.

The Mass Sung in Heaven

Just as Gertrud's death itself seems endlessly deferred, so too is the conclusion of the *The Herald*, even though chapter 36 ends with a doxology and the traditional request for prayers from the scribe. It is appropriate that *The Mass Personally Sung in Heaven by the Lord Jesus for a Certain Virgin Called Trutta While She Was Still Alive* should follow Book 5, for even though this vision took place, as the title stresses, "while she was still alive," it is indeed the missing account of Gertrud's personal glorification in heaven. During the Mass, chanted and chosen (after some discussion) by Christ himself, Gertrud's sins are forgiven, she is escorted by angels, presented to the Holy Trinity, and enthroned. At the appropriate moment Christ sacrifices himself on the altar of his divine heart as the heavenly Mass proceeds in parallel to the conventual Mass that Gertrud was (as so often) unable to attend: "In that very same time that the Son of God offered his divine heart to God the Father, the bell was ringing in the church at the elevation of the Host. So it came about that at one and the same moment the Lord was accomplishing in heaven what the service of the priest was doing on earth" (*Mass*, 12). Christ then instructs Gertrud to recite the Lord's Prayer and to pray for the church. Then, "calling her to him, and pressing her in his bosom with lovely embraces, and smothering her with sweetest kisses, he flowed into her with such great condescension, wonderfully penetrating her with the power of his divine nature. . . . And thus he united her to himself sacramentally in such a union by the reception of his most holy Body and Blood" (*Mass*, 13). After a final blessing, Gertrud emerges from her state of ecstasy but is still conscious of a continuing union with the Lord: "coming to herself, she was aware of her beloved held close by an indissoluble union in her inmost being" (*Mass*, 15).

The Herald of God's Loving-Kindness and the *Book of Special Grace*

We can deduce from *Special Grace* II.42 and V.24 that Gertrud and another Helfta nun (almost certainly Sister N.) compiled this book containing the revelations of Mechtild of Hackeborn, younger sister of the abbess Gertrud; Mechtild was the monastery's chantress, and Gertrud's novice-mistress and spiritual confidante. This is of particular relevance for Book 5 of *The Herald*, the structure and content of which overlap with parts of *The Book of Special Grace*.

The structure of *The Book of Special Grace* V displays some interesting similarities to that of Book 5 of *The Herald*. Both open with accounts of the life and death of the abbess Gertrud, Mechtild's elder sister, then follow with the deaths and *post mortem* fates of various other women, mainly nuns, associated with Helfta (LDP V.2–10 and *Special Grace* V.3–6). Apart from the abbess the only woman who appears in both texts is Mechtild of Magdebourg (LDP V.7 and *Special Grace* V.6), but the accounts are quite different.

Chapters concerned with men follow in both, though the emphases are different: lay brothers in LDP V.11–5, but male religious, including the Dominican friars Albert the Great (d. 1280) and Thomas Aquinas (d. 1274), in *Special Grace* V.7–9. LDP next describes the release of an anonymous soul (V.16), while *Special Grace* follows with the souls of two laymen (V.10–11), including Helfta's founder, Count Burchard of Mansfeld, then of various others, including a little girl (V.12), and Solomon, Samson, Origen, and Trajan (V.16).

LDP V.17, on the release of souls of relatives through the prayers of the Helfta nuns, parallels *Special Grace* V.14, on souls freed through Mechtild's prayers. LDP V.18 and 19, on the Great Psalter devotion and its efficacy, parallel *Special Grace* V.18, on the prayer *Fons vivus*, and V.19, on the efficacy of reciting five Pater Nosters. LDP V.22, on the punishments endured by murmurers and the disobedient, parallels *Special Grace* V.20, on purgatory and hell.

As we have seen, LDP V.33–36 concern the book itself, its authenticity, its title, and its offering to and acceptance by the Lord; *Special Grace* V.22 and 24 are also concerned with that book's authenticity and its title, and, much later, *Special Grace* V.31 records the writers' thanksgiving for its completion and Mechtild's vision of the Lord's claiming ownership. However, apart from this chapter, *Special Grace* V.25–33 seem unrelated to LDP V,[14] and conversely LDP V.23–32, about a third of the whole and the section detailing Gertrud's longing for and preparation for death, find no parallel in *Special Grace*. Nonetheless it looks as if LDP took some fundamental ideas for the structuring of its Book 5 from the parallel book in *Special Grace*. This is not surprising, given that Sister N. and Gertrud were involved in the composition of both.

The Abbess Gertrud in LDP and *The Book of Special Grace*

But there is an even closer relationship between LDP V.1 and V.4, and *Special Grace* VI and VII. The two texts concerned with the abbess Gertrud, LDP V.1 and *Special Grace* VI, share material: of the latter's nine chapters, most of chapters 1, 4, 5, and 6 are very similar verbally to material found in LDP V.1.1. In addition to this common core, each text has unique material reflecting its own perspective. In LDP Gertrud's role as visionary is foregrounded. She is the intermediary of the divine, recognised as such by the community and her superiors, including the abbess (see, for instance, LDP V.1.7, lines 1–6, V.1.10, lines 1–7, and V.1.12, lines 1–4).

Special Grace in contrast never portrays Gertrud in this light, as its focus is on Mechtild of Hackeborn. Indeed, although we know that

---

14. The best manuscript of *Special Grace* lacks V.27–29.

Gertrud was heavily involved in its compilation, it never mentions her by name at all. This self-effacement can be extreme: in *Special Grace* VI.6 we are told of the response chanted immediately after the abbess's death but not given the revealing detail, to be gleaned from LDP V.1.24, that Gertrud herself intoned it. Presumably she was deputizing for Mechtild, who was the chantress but sick at the time of her sister's death. This is the only evidence we have of Gertrud's holding any official position at Helfta.

Similarly, LDP describes the dramatic moment, which only a visionary could witness, when the abbess's soul left her body and flew up to heaven: "that happy soul, a hundredfold blessed, was raised up by jubilation of inestimable delight to that uniquely excellent tabernacle, that is, the sweetest heart of Jesus, opened up to her so faithfully, generously, and joyfully, as had been shown to <Gertrud> during the previous day" (V.1.23).

The final clause refers to the end of LDP V.1.20, which describes how the Lord leaned over the dying abbess, opening his heart with both hands and stretching it over her. Although we are not explicitly told that it was Gertrud who witnessed this, this account must surely depend on her testimony as visionary. *Special Grace* VI.6 gives a virtually identical account: "That happy soul, a hundredfold blessed, flew up with inestimable jubilation of delight to that uniquely excellent tabernacle, that is, the sweetest heart of Jesus, opened up so faithfully and joyfully to her."

But *Special Grace* VI contains much that is not found in LDP V.1. Not surprisingly, most of this describes Mechtild's prayers for her sister and her interactions with the Lord on her behalf: in other words, Mechtild is shown as fulfilling a role similar to that played by Gertrud in LDP's version. For instance, part of *Special Grace* VI.1 and VI.2–3 describes several extended visions experienced by Mechtild concerning her sister during the twenty-two weeks that intervened between the abbess's stroke and her death. These include lengthy dialogues with the Lord in a vein familiar to readers of both *Special Grace* and LDP.

Nonetheless, about two-thirds of the account of the abbess's actual death is common to both LDP V.1.23–24 and *Special Grace* VI.6. But the textual relationship between the two is complex. Here is the opening sentence of *Special Grace* VI.1: "Lady Gertrud, our abbess of sweetest memory, glorious and truly brilliant light of our church, who blossomed like a rose in all the virtues, exemplar of complete sanctity and a most solid pillar of true religion, was sister in the flesh of this blessed virgin of whom we have written." This skillfully weaves together phrases and sentences that appear dispersed in LDP V.1. Its opening phrase echoes LDP's title, "The glorious death of the reverend Lady G<ertrud>, abbess, of sweetest memory"; "who blossomed like a rose in all the virtues" is a condensation of "in these and various other, or, rather, all virtues she blossomed like a rose all her life" (LDP V.1.2); and "a most solid pillar of true religion" recalls "her decisions and precedents should be like most solid pillars to uphold the religious life" (LDP V.1.6).

Special Grace continues, "She conducted herself so laudably, gently, and prudently in this office that she was held in great reverence and loved by all with the love bestowed on a mother, showing herself both to God and to men and women as lovable and full of grace." This combines "wisely, gently, and prudently" (LDP V.1.1) and "so that she showed herself both to God and to men and women wonderfully lovable and full of grace" (LDP V.1.2). A few sentences later, we are told about the abbess's personal and physical care for the sick, in "serving them with her own hands, both for their rest and for their refreshment," which echoes LDP's "by helping with her own hands, obtaining for them what they needed, both for their rest and for their refreshment" (LDP V.1.1). The next sentence describes the abbess after her stroke: "when she could not speak, she showed them such sincere compassion by gesture and nods that she moved very many to tears." This echoes a quite different passage from LDP: "she displayed so sincere an emotion of compassion by gesture and nods that she moved the hardest hearts to tears" (LDP V.1.16).

Is *Special Grace* plundering LDP, or is the debt in the other direction? Neither, perhaps. Rather, we might postulate a prolific but somewhat harried compiler (Sister N.), with many other responsibilities elsewhere in the community,[15] seizing the opportunity to recycle and adapt what she has written earlier but not always remembering accurately. Alternatively, she could well have been working on *Special Grace* and LDP simultaneously and have almost unconsciously echoed her own phrasing.

Mechtild of Hackeborn in LDP and *The Book of Special Grace*

The situation with regard to LDP V.4 and *Special Grace* VII on Mechtild is somewhat different. The LDP account of Mechtild's sickness, death, and apotheosis begins just a month before her death, while *Special Grace* VI offers a longer perspective, beginning with a declaration that Mechtild had been a nun for fifty-seven years and was very ill for about three years before she died. (Perhaps this indicates that *Special Grace* was designed for a wider audience than just the Helfta community, who would already know that kind of detail.) But from here on the two narratives are very close, extending from the last time in her life that Mechtild received the sacrament, on the penultimate Sunday of the liturgical year, up until her requiem Mass. From the day after her death, however (*Special Grace* VII.14 onwards, LDP V.4.21), there is no overlap.

The compilers used more than one informant for *Special Grace* VII.1 and 2, unlike LDP V.4, which is solely dependent on Gertrud. In *Special Grace* VII.1 "a person devoutly attentive to God," probably Gertrud herself, is cited as the source of information for a dialogue with Christ. But the opening of the following chapter refers to "another woman," presumably another visionary nun, who hears the Lord summoning Mechtild with the words of the Song of Songs. However, much of *Special Grace* VII.3–13 is clearly reliant on Gertrud. *Special*

---

15. Sister N. might have been one of the schoolmistresses that the abbess Gertrud provided to improve the novices' Latin; in addition, her careful use of medical and physiological terms suggests that she was involved with the care of the sick.

Grace VII.3 corresponds to some of LDP V.4.4, with an instructive if puzzling difference. This is the only time that both texts give an account of the same vision, and they relate how "a person, devoutly praying" (*Special Grace* VII.3), who is clearly identified by LDP as Gertrud, received a revelation that she should warn Mechtild to prepare for the sacrament of the anointing of the sick. But in *Special Grace* a similar revelation is also made "to another person," and the narrator points out the importance of *two* witnesses.[16] Why is there an unnamed second witness, to whose presence the reader's attention is so carefully drawn, in *Special Grace* but not in LDP?

Possibly Gertrud decreed, out of humility, that *Special Grace* should use witnesses other than herself when available, and their existence certainly throws light on the Helfta community as a whole and its normalization, even popularization, of mystical experience. This is also in evidence at the beginning of the following chapter, *Special Grace* VII.4, which recounts the anointing of Mechtild and corresponds to LDP V.4.5 and V.4.6 except for its first sentence: this introduces a revelation made to no fewer than three people: "It was revealed to three persons that the Lord was most courteously present in the form of an elegant spouse and was himself offering the life-giving sacrament to his chosen." (From the sentence that follows, and from LDP V.4.5, it is clear that one of these three is Gertrud.)

Special Grace VII.7 is missing from the Wolfenbüttel manuscript, so Paquelin boldly translated it into Latin "from an old German edition," that is, presumably, from the German translation of *Special Grace* printed in Leipzig in 1503. As he noted, though, the missing chapter does occur in LDP, as parts of LDP V.4.8–11. He speculated that *Special Grace* omitted the chapter out of respect for Gertrud, as part of it shows her in an unfavorable light: in LDP V.4.10, out of humility, she decides not to make known to the community what is divinely revealed to her about the dying Mechtild. But God makes clear his displeasure by temporarily depriving her of this privileged knowledge, so that she

---

16. Compare LDP I.2.1, lines 8–10.

"could not perceive a single thing of what was happening to the sick woman until she acknowledged her guilt and, washing it away by repenting, promised the Lord that she would willingly make known whatever he deigned to reveal to her." This does not explain why Sister N. had no problem including the episode in LDP, though perhaps it was at Gertrud's own insistence as, once more, only she can be its source.

Special Grace VII.13, which corresponds almost verbatim to LDP V.4.21, is the last chapter common to the texts. It relates a characteristically Gertrudian vision of the divine heart received during Mechtild's requiem Mass. From this point, as noted earlier, the two texts diverge. LDP contains just two more sections (V.4.22 and 23) that describe visions relating to prayers performed and Masses offered by Gertrud and other members of the community for Mechtild's glorified soul, and the celestial benefits these have won her and others. The chronology is quite vague, both visions taking place simply "on another occasion." Characteristically Gertrudian floral imagery figures prominently in both. Possibly Sister N. curtailed the Mechtild material at this point because she knew more was already available in *Special Grace*, or would be in the future. For in contrast the latter has no fewer than nine further chapters, most but not all of which must depend on the testimony of Gertrud, who as witness to events in heaven is several times described as "she who saw these things."

To summarize at the risk of over-simplifying, then, *Special Grace* VII.3–13 overlap with LDP V.3–21 but have nothing to correspond to LDP's two opening and two closing paragraphs. Conversely, LDP V.4.3–21, focusing almost exclusively on what could be known to Gertrud, have practically nothing to correspond to *Special Grace* VII.1–2 or 14–22. The two texts share a common core, but their beginnings and endings are different, just as their purposes are different. It would probably have been easier to adapt *Special Grace* VII as LDP V.4 than vice versa, as it would mainly just require excising any visionary material that did not derive from Gertrud and writing very short opening and closing sections. It is therefore possible that *Special Grace* VII was written first, by Sister N. and Gertrud herself, and later adapted by the former for the five-book version of the LDP.

A Final Note on the Texts

At present we know of only two manuscripts containing all five books of LDP: Munich, BSB Clm 15332, dated 1413, and Vienna, ONB, Cod. 4224, dated 1485 and 1490. Book 5 is also found in the recently discovered Harvard manuscript, Houghton Library, MS Riant 90, which is almost certainly the second half of Darmstadt, Universitäts- und Landesbibliothek, MS 84. Book 5 was edited from the Vienna manuscript by Louis Paquelin in the nineteenth century, and from the two complete manuscripts for the SCh edition, from which this translation has been made.

The Mass Personally Sung in Heaven by the Lord Jesus for a Certain Virgin Called Trutta While She Was Still Alive has a more complex textual history. It follows immediately after the end of Book 5 in both Munich, BSB Clm 15332, and Vienna, ONB, Cod. 4224. In Bonn, Universitäts- und Landesbibliothek, S 0726, an early fifteenth-century manuscript, it occurs as an independent text on fols. 361ra–364vb.[17] In Houghton Library, MS Riant 90, it precedes Book 4. In the first printed edition of the Latin (1536) it is placed between Books 4 and 5 and it was printed in the same position by Paquelin and numbered as a continuation of Book 4. The SCh edition has restored it to its proper place after Book 5.

The textual basis of *Special Grace* VI and VII is very slender: only one manuscript, Wolfenbüttel, Cod. Guelf. 1003 Helmst., dated 1370 on fol. 204^{v}, contains both. Its account of Mechtild's death, described as "[liber] sextus de extremis felicis sororis Mechthildis gloriose virginis sanctimonialis in Helfede," "the sixth [book] concerning the death of the glorious virgin, blessed sister Mechtild, nun at Helfta," occupies fols. 182^{r}–193^{v}. This is followed by the account of the abbess Gertrud's life and death, the scribe handling the transition as follows:

> Explicit liber de extremis beate virginis sororis Mechthildis
> de Helfede. Incipit nunc de laudabi[fol. 194^{v}]li vita et morte
> venerabilis domine Gerdrudis abbatisse sororis sue.

---

17. Nemes, "Text Production and Authorship," 107.

Here ends the book concerning the death of the blessed virgin, sister Mechtild of Helfta. Now here begins [the book] concerning the life and death of the venerable Lady abbess Gertrud, her sister.

It is therefore arguable that this account of Mechtild's death is an integral part of *Special Grace*, because it is described as the "sixth book," but that the account of the abbess's life and death is actually a separate text.

Additional evidence for the independent status of the account of the abbess Gertrud comes from the late-thirteenth- or early-fourteenth-century Leipzig, Universitätsbibliothek MS 671.[18] This is the only other *Special Grace* manuscript to contain an account of the death of Mechtild, where it appears as a separate text on fols. 211^v–225^r, following I–V, which occupy fols. 6^v–211^v. Entitled *De vita et conversatione laudabilis domine Gertrudis abbatissae*, it also includes *Special Grace* V.1 and 2 (two visions of the abbess glorified in heaven). There is no other manuscript witness for *Special Grace* VI or VII.

Paquelin, the only (relatively) modern editor, decided to treat both as integral parts of *Special Grace*. In addition he reversed the manuscript order, so that the death of Mechtild became Part Seven, and the life and death of the abbess Part Six. He gave no reason for this somewhat cavalier editorial decision, and one can only presume that he thought the climax and conclusion of *Special Grace* should be Mechtild's passing rather than that of her sister.

18. Paquelin gave no shelf mark for this manuscript (followed by Voaden 2010, 442, and 449). I should like to thank the Leipzig Universitätsbibliothek staff, who provided the shelf mark, a recent, unpublished, catalogue description, and digital images of the manuscript, which for conservation reasons cannot be consulted at present.

THE HERALD OF GOD'S LOVING-KINDNESS

Book 5

PROLOGUE

The Lord quite often reveals the rewards of the departed for the salvation of the living, so that they may choose examples, either of recompense for what has been done or of avoidance of what should be eschewed. We have therefore written down in one place material concerning certain souls whose merits and rewards the Lord condescended to reveal to Gertrud: first, concerning the most glorious and amiable reverend Lady G<ertrud>, most kindly abbess, whose deeds, though difficult to imitate, it is pious to admire, and to give devout thanks for her to God, who condescended to bestow upon her every good thing. Amen.

CHAPTER ONE

THE GLORIOUS DEATH OF THE REVEREND LADY G<ERTRUD>, ABBESS, OF SWEETEST MEMORY[1]

1. Truly worthy and filled with the Holy Spirit, of reverend memory and to be embraced in the arms of unfeigned love, Lady G<ertrud>, whom we should revere as most kindly abbess and worthy of all praise and honor, governed the abbey for forty years and eleven days. She did so wisely, gently, and prudently, with wonderful discretion, to the praise of God and the profit of men and women: with the most fervent love and devotion with respect to God, in the greatest loving-kindness and solicitude with respect to her neighbor, foremost in humility and affliction with respect to herself. Displaying humility in her deeds, most conscientious in visiting the sick and, by helping with her own hands, obtaining for them what they needed, both for their rest and for their refreshment, and whatever else was necessary, from which her subordinates' vehement affections could not deter her. Not only in this but also in such other things as cleaning the cloister and setting things to rights, she was sometimes the first, or even quite often the only one to set to work until she persuaded, or rather

1. The abbess died in 1291.

5

attracted her subordinates by her example or her gentle words to help her.

2. Although in these and various other, or, rather, all virtues she blossomed like a rose all her life, so much so that she showed herself both to God and to men and women wonderfully lovable and full of grace, finally, after forty years and eleven days (as I said above), alas! alas! alas! she fell sick with what is called a minor stroke.[2] This dart was sent from the hand of the Almighty to draw to himself this noble soul abounding in the fruits of so many virtues and to bring her out of the battlefield of physical misery, but all those who knew her could conceive how profoundly this pierced the innermost being of those subject to her. For we found it unthinkable that throughout the length and breadth of the whole world a person could be found who would be *prevented in* so ample *blessing* by God,* both in gifts of nature and of grace, and also of fortune in things related to the divine.

*see Ps 20:4

For although the number of people whom her maternal care had received and nurtured in religion had far exceeded one hundred, we have never heard from any of them that they could find someone for whom they could have greater affection and whom they would prefer to her in anything—so much so that, in addition, wonderful to relate! When children under the age of seven were sometimes received into the monastery, although they did not as yet have the natural intelligence to understand those things that are God's, nonetheless as soon as they were able to recognize, at first in a childish way, that she was their mother in a special sense, they rested on her gentle kindliness with so much affection that

---

2. *apoplexia minor*, a technical medieval Latin medical term.

they thought it ridiculous that they had ever declared
that they loved their father or mother or any other of
their relatives more than they loved her. Since it would
take far too long to recount these stories and others like
them, and especially what outsiders felt about her when
they saw her and heard her words, all redolent with
wisdom, let us pour back all things, with praise and
thanksgiving, into that abyss from whose outflowing
all good proceeds.

3. Since, then, that sunbeam was moving through
bodily sickness towards the sunset of death, her daughters feared lest perhaps it might happen that, having lost
the splendor of such shining examples and the help of
such a loving mother's leadership, they might at some
time go astray in the path of the religious life, with all
their heart's affection they fled to *the Father of mercies,**   *2 Cor 1:3
praying for her restoration to health with such prayers
as they could offer. Because he is the highest good,
from which every good receives its goodness, he did not
*despise the supplication of the poor,** and also because   *Ps 21:25
it was not fitting to grant them an outcome contrary to
the divine plan concerning their mother's health, he
nonetheless granted the outcome that her daughters were
consoled, rejoicing in the blessedness of their mother.
And so through \<Gertrud\> he gave consoling replies to
those constantly praying for her, as will become clear
in what follows.

4. On one occasion, when \<Gertrud\> was praying
for her and longed to know her state, the Lord replied,
"With inestimable joy have I waited for this moment *to
lead* my chosen one *into the wilderness,* so that I might
there *speak to her heart.** I am *not defrauded of* my   *see Hos 2:14
desire,** for she herself is responding according to my   *see Ps 77:30
most acceptable good pleasure, and she is obeying me
in all things according to my sweetest delight." That

is, the "wilderness" is the sickness in which the Lord speaks to the heart, and not to the ear, of his beloved, because his speech cannot be understood in a human way, just as those things that are spoken to the heart are sensed rather than heard. Thence the Lord's "words" to his chosen are trials and heaviness of heart, as when the sick person thinks that he is useless and wasting his time uselessly, and that others toiling for him are also wasting their time, for the enjoyment of good health will perhaps never come.

To this the chosen one responds according to God's excellent pleasure, since, keeping patience in her heart, she desires that the Lord's will should be completely accomplished in her. For such a response is not heard in heaven in a human way, but it resounds, as if through the sweetest divine instrument, that is, the heart of Jesus Christ, in the highest delight of the whole Trinity and of all the court of heaven. For no human heart on earth could offer its willingness to endure according to God's will while experiencing heavy burdens, if that ability had not flowed into it from that most perfect heart of Jesus Christ. Thence it must always resound in heaven through that heart, the heart of Jesus Christ.

5. The Lord added, "My chosen one obeys me according to my sweetest delight when she does not despise the burdens of sickness as Queen Vashti despised the authority of King Ahasuerus when he ordered her to enter *with the crown set upon her head, to show her* *see Esth 1:11 *beauty to the princes*.* So when I delight to show the loveliness of my chosen one in the presence of the Trinity, ever to be worshiped, and the whole court of heaven, then I weigh her down greatly with both sickness and exhaustion, and she serves me according to the sweetest delight of my heart when she then patiently accepts relief and physical necessities with discretion. And

her occasional reluctance to do such things takes the place of a jewel in her crown. But it is right for her to accept comfort, recalling that *to them that love <me> all things work together unto good** through my most kindly loving-kindness."

*Rom 8:28

6. Then another time while G<ertrud> was again praying for her, the Lord replied, "I sometimes take pleasure in my chosen one's preparing gifts for me, and then I give her pearls and flowers of gold. That is, pearls are the senses, and flowers of gold the leisure with which she is preparing adornments most fitting and acceptable to me when, having some leisure and having somewhat recovered her strength, she attends to her duties as far as she can, concerned with how she should make determinations that can strengthen and sustain the religious life, so that after her death her decisions and precedents should be like most solid pillars to uphold the religious life to my eternal praise. But when she works at this, if she feels her health endangered, she immediately stops, and entrusts the task to me with the confidence that I will complete it. For this is the trust that moves my divine heart: when she feels better, she tries to do what she can with respect to her duties, and when she feels worse, she immediately stops again and trusts in me."

7. Another time when Lady Gertrud, the abbess of sweet memory, was more especially weighed down because she could not do anything with her hands, and thence feared that she was spending her time uselessly, with her accustomed humility she sought reassurance from <Gertrud>, whose response she preferred to others. She entrusted to her the task of praying to the Lord on this. When she was devoutly doing this, she received this answer from the Lord: "A kindly king would never question his chosen one if she neglected to arrange her

jewels at the moment when she delighted to stretch out her hands in a caress. But it would be the more welcome because in all kinds of things she was always prepared to be subject to his will. Therefore the sweetness of my most kindly heart welcomes it so much the more if that chosen one patiently bears the difficulties of sickness. And as soon as she feels an improvement, she goes back to her wish to promote the religious life insofar as she can, without making her sickness worse."

8. Again, while she wanted to resign her position as abbess because of her sickness, as she thought that she could not accomplish anything useful in office, and on this too asked <Gertrud> about the divine will, the Lord instructed her with these words: "I am sanctifying my chosen one by that sickness so that she may dwell with me, just as a church is sanctified by the bishop's consecration. Again, just as a church is strengthened with bars to prevent the entrance of the unworthy, so I am barring her too, lest her outer senses might receive such varied things, in which there is sometimes no great utility, and nonetheless they disturb the heart, and also sometimes make it pay less attention to me. Thence speaking in the book of Wisdom and saying, *My delights are to be with the children of men,** I have rendered her so that because of the burdens of sickness it is right that I should dwell in her, according to those words, *The Lord is nigh unto those that are of troubled heart.**

9. "In addition I have so added adornment in good intentions and good will that, resting in her like a king on his most tranquil bed, I could for a while enjoy my delights in her according to my best pleasure on earth, before I conduct her to eternal delights in heaven. Indeed, I have left her external faculties quite healthy in part, so that I may make known my replies and my will through her to the daughters of the community subject

*Prov 8:31

*Ps 33:19

to her, just as I had once given the ark of the covenant to the children of Israel as an oracle, that they might honor me in her.* May she, like the ark, contain manna,† that is, sweetness of consolation, in her heart and also in her words, according to her ability, for all those subject to her. Let her have *the stone tables of testimony*,* that is, let her teach what should be done and what should be forgone according to her own good pleasure, insofar as she can discern it herself. Let her also contain *the rod of Aaron*,* that is, the correction of the wicked, imposing penance by discernment with promptness of spirit, recalling that I could myself correct all things left uncorrected either by inspiration or by trial, but in what I do through her agency, I increase her reward. But if those whom she corrects are not corrected, this will not damage her, since she has displayed such loving care. For human beings can plant and water, but I alone can give *the increase*."*

*see Num 7:89
†see Exod 16:33-34
*see Exod 31:18

*Num 17:10

*see 1 Cor 3:6

10. Similarly, when she feared to act negligently in omitting holy communion and prayers and other spiritual exercises, and thence feared to receive communion unworthily, since because of her sickness she could not prepare herself for holy communion with any exercises, she was privileged to be instructed and consoled by the Lord through <Gertrud> as follows: "When she omits communion, or something similar that she would willingly do but feels it would harm her, purely on my account, then my most generous loving-kindness wishes to give her its own share [of merit], in place of her own share that she loses, just as whatever good is done in the whole church is my own."

11. Just as it is the mark of virtuous souls to fear guilt where there is none,[3] so she was weighed down at

---

3. Gregory the Great, Epp XI.64 (PL 77:1195B); see also IV.4.8.

one time because she considered that those serving her were wasting their time, since good health would not result. God, who is faithful and *will not suffer anyone*
*see
1 Cor 10:13
to be tempted above that he is able,* consoled her with these words through <Gertrud> on this matter too: "Let her be served with reverence and kindness, care and good humor for my love and honor, for I am God and, dwelling in her, have appointed her the head of the community; thence everyone is bound to support her, as the limbs support the head. And let her accept it to my honor, rejoicing that I am increasing the merits of my chosen through her, as through a more faithful friend, while I shall reward each and every benefit bestowed on her, not only by actions but also by affection or words, as if they had been bestowed on me."

12. Similarly, on Saint Leafwine's day[4] the whole community was collectively praying for her, that she should be healed through the merits of that saint. That same blessed martyr, invoked rather pressingly by <Gertrud>, seemed to give her this answer: "Since it is the king's pleasure to caress his chosen one in private, what knight could possibly demand of the king that he send her out to comfort her household by her presence? So it is not appropriate for anyone to demand her return to health, as through patience and good will her sickness is one with God and is, as it were, a loving caress for the King of heaven." From this it should be known that when those whose sickness is more precious to God call upon the saints' assistance, they deserve to receive this: God's grace, gently flowing into them, renders them

---

4. November 12: the Yorkshireman Saint Leafwine or Lebuin, d. ca.733, associate of Saint Boniface, who evangelized the Saxons and Frisians.

more patient, and thence from their sickness they bear
fruit that is more abundant and more precious to God.

13. These witnesses are indeed most trustworthy: all
those should confess it who, recognizing God's grace in
that sickness, contemplated the quality of her life. For
she lost the power of speech for twenty-two weeks, so
much so that she could not indicate her requirements by
any word or even gestures, except by these two words
alone: "My spirit." When those present did not understand what she meant by this, and did not do what she
wanted, that blessed mother struggled at length, repeating "My spirit," to no avail. Finally, *dumb as a gentle
lamb,** and looking with dove-like gaze at those things   *see Isa 53:7
that were being done against her wishes, she sometimes
laughed most kindly and could never be thought to have
fallen into impatience. From the root of love of God and
neighbor, which had been deeply embedded in her inmost being all her life, this too was clear in her sickness:
that she was never so unwell that she did not become
livelier, as if there were nothing wrong with her, when
she heard talk, or just a word, about God.

14. It was also clear how very great was this devotion that she possessed from the tears that she shed
so copiously when about to receive communion, and
from other signs of eagerness that were evident in her
when hearing Mass. She always wanted to be taken
there, though one of her legs was as if already dead, and
when she leaned on it, it was so unbearably painful that
it seemed a miracle that she could endure the slightest
touch on that leg on which she stood. But she gave no
hint of pain, lest she should no longer be permitted to
go to Mass. Concerning the canonical Hours she was
astonishingly conscientious and devout, so much so that
when she was drowsy from her sickness or sometimes
had food in her mouth or a cup at her lips to drink from,

nonetheless at the time of the Hours she always forced herself to be miraculously alert. The last "My spirit" that we heard her say was requesting the recitation of Compline, after which she began her death agony.

15. She showed herself perfect in love of neighbor by her liberal kindliness, for although, as I said earlier, she could say nothing except "My spirit," with that phrase she did most completely all that was needed: receiving those coming through the door and lovingly extending the one hand that she could scarcely move, caressing those who were present and responding to all that she was asked, gently touching their chin or hands, so much so that the older people declared that they could never grow tired of her company, but took more delight in it than with anyone else who bestowed on them truly delightful conversation or an outstanding gift. As they left, she farewelled them with the same phrase, that is, "My spirit," raising her damaged arm to bless them so kindly that it was indeed delightful to behold.

16. When she learned that one of her daughters was confined to bed and was said to be growing worse, even though she could not take a single step or speak a word except, as we have said so often, "My spirit," nonetheless she did her best to show by her gestures such a strong desire to visit the sick woman that those present could not refuse to take her there. When she had arrived, she displayed so sincere an emotion of compassion by gesture and nods that she moved the hardest hearts to tears. And since no pen is sufficient to make plain each and every one of her virtues and the distinguishing marks of her loving-kindness, let us offer to the giver

*Ps 49:14   of all good things *the sacrifice of praise** for them all, from the depths of our being.

17. Since, as can be gleaned from what has already been said, she miraculously spoke this phrase, "My

spirit," so easily, and repeated it so constantly, and uttered nothing else at all that was comprehensible, <Gertrud>, who loved her dearly, asked the Lord what it meant. On this she was instructed by the Lord with these words: "I, God dwelling in her, have drawn her spirit to me and united it with me so that in all creation she desired me alone; therefore in speaking, asking and requesting what she needs, she makes mention of my spirit, in which her spirit lives. And as often as she does this, I indicate to all the heavenly court that she is intent on me alone; from this she will have eternal glory in heaven."

18. Very many similar testimonies could be recorded of the happy state of our most blessed mother, revealed to this daughter of hers by the Lord, but for the sake of brevity I will pass them over. For they all agree on this, and point at this: that what we have seen with our own eyes bears witness, while Holy Scripture demonstrates most openly, that God was indeed dwelling in her and with her, and that he directed all that happened to her by his sweetest spirit according to his pleasure.

19. About a month after her loss of speech, she was so unwell one morning that she was thought to be dying. When the community had been summoned and she was being urgently anointed, the Lord appeared in the form of a bridegroom in all his beauty, as Bernard says,[5] stretching out his arms as if to embrace her and looking at her tenderly and, wherever she turned, placing himself opposite the sick woman's face. Through this Gertrud perceived that the Lord was swayed by such sweetness of love for his beloved that, as if longing to take her to himself in this act of preparation,[6] that is,

---

5. SC 32.3 (SBOp 1:227, line 27).
6. That is, the sacrament of anointing.

with hands outstretched to embrace her, in some way
he was anticipating her death with strong desire, even
though she lived for more than four months after this.
And when she asked how our reverend mother and lady,
the subject of this essay, could compare with the rewards
of blessed virgins who were already canonized and had
shed their blood for the faith, the Lord replied, "In the
first year of her rule she united her will to mine, and
with my assistance, in all that she did she was shown
capable of equaling the rewards of those crowned most
lavishly. But now I have added as many rewards to her
glory as the number of additional years, accompanied
by growth in virtue, that I have granted her." From this
anyone may consider with what dazzling glory God's
chosen one, our most kindly mother, is crowned!

20. And so that day arrived, for which God's chosen
one had longed with so many joyful desires and had secured with so many devout prayers, on which she began
her death-agony; the Lord was seen to come quickly, all
blithe,[7] accompanied on his right and on his left by his
most blessed mother and the beloved disciple, John the
Evangelist. After them followed a countless multitude of
both men and women, from the whole court of heaven,
and specially the army of purest white virgins,[8] which

7. *festivus*: compare *mitis atque festivus Christi Iesu tibi as-
pectus appareat, qui te inter assistentes sibi iugiter interesse
decernat*, "May Christ Jesus appear to you with a mild and blithe
countenance, and give you a place among those who are to be in
his presence forever," from the prayer *Commendo te* in the order
for commendation of a soul.

8. Adapted from *candidatorum tibi Martyrum triumphator
exercitus obviet; . . . iubilantium te Virginum chorus excipiat*,
"the triumphant army of purest white martyrs will meet you . . .
the choir of joyous virgins will receive you," from the prayer
Commendo te.

seemed to fill that house during that day on which she suffered her death agony. They seemed to mingle with the community, which also remained there throughout the whole day, bewailing their desolation with tears and sighs, commending to God the passing of so beloved a mother with devout prayers. Indeed, when the Lord Jesus had come to the bed of his beloved, he seemed to caress her with exceedingly sweet gestures capable of worthily assuaging the bitterness of death. And when the words *And bowing his head he gave up the ghost** were read in   *John 19:30 the passion before the sick woman, as if from excess of love the Lord Jesus leaned over the dying woman, opened his own heart with both hands, and stretched it over her.

21. And when the whole community was at prayer, <Gertrud,> once again guided by sweet love, said to the Lord, "Ah, most kindly Jesu, for the sake of your unfailing loving-kindness, by which you gave us so lovable a mother, since you now intend to receive her, swayed by our tears and sighs, as far as it is possible, treat her like your mother by showing her some of that love that you showed your own most blessed mother when she was leaving the body." At this, moved by loving compassion, the Lord seemed to say to his mother, "Tell me, lady mother, what I did for you on earth while you were leaving the body that you found delightful? For this woman is asking me to act as I did to my own mother!" Then the most merciful Virgin kindly replied, "My son, I took great pleasure in finding such a safe refuge in your arms." The Lord replied, "You received this, my mother, because you so often honored my passion on earth with sorrowful sighs." And the Lord added, "To deserve this reward, my chosen one will make up for it by suffering throughout this day, drawing her breath with difficulty as many times as you breathed forth sighs on earth while recalling my passion."

22. Thus she endured her death-agony throughout the day. During that time, in her enjoyment of the divine loving-kindness, she was brought delightful flowers from the divine heart, open before her, as if from a garden or from a storehouse of perfumed spices. Moment by moment there appeared heavenly spirits, leaning from heaven to earth and gazing at her, to sing this song with sweetest melody as her invitation: "Come, come, come, lady, for heavenly delights await you. Alleluia, alleluia."

23. And so that most delicious hour was at hand at which that heavenly bridegroom, the imperial Son of the highest Father, determined to receive his beloved, emerging from the prison of the world, as she had long desired, to rest with him in the wedding-chamber of love. As he drew near her, <Gertrud> heard him say these honey-sweet words to her: "Behold, now I shall make you mine at last through a kiss of most potent delight, and I shall present you to the Lord God my heavenly Father in the most straight embrace of my divine heart," as if to say, Although my omnipotence has sustained you until this moment to win further merit, the ardor of my fastidious love, unable to bear it any longer, will present you to me, by releasing you, my longed-for treasure, from the flesh, to assuage the unrestraint of my most ardent love towards you, for the pleasure of my sweetest delights. When he had said this, having left the prison of the flesh that happy soul, a hundredfold blessed, was raised up by jubilation of inestimable delight to that uniquely excellent tabernacle; that is, the sweetest heart of Jesus opened up to he so faithfully, generously, and joyfully, as had been shown to <Gertrud> during the previous day.

What human being can guess what there she sensed, what saw, what heard, what inhaled[9] with blessed love

9. Compare LDP II.8.5, lines 11–12.

from the overflow of the divine loving-kindness—she who deserved so wonderful a steed by special privilege?[10] Human weakness cannot haltingly describe with what honey-sweet caresses in the sweetest depths of her being the vigorous and refined bridegroom conducted her, and with what joyful dance those companions welcomed her with joyous crowns, at the very moment that the glorification of so happy a soul was accomplished with the festive praises of all! It therefore befits us, together with the citizens of heaven, who were privileged to take a blessed part in these events, to sing a song of jubilation with thanksgiving to God, the creator of all.

24. Therefore since that blazing sun, which used to scatter its rays far and wide in our world, had set, and that tiny drop had happily found once again the depths from which it had flowed, her daughters were left alone in lonely darkness. Lifting up eyes of faith to the glory of their mother's blessedness through the aperture of hope, as if through the most narrow cracks[11] of sorrow, then did they truly pour forth tears from the heart as an offering for so kindly a mother: they had never seen one like her, nor did they expect to do so.[12] Nonetheless, with loud voices they uttered praises to heaven, amidst heavenly gladness from joy in their mother's glory, and

---

10. *vehiculum*, any means of conveyance. The term also appears in V.24.2 and 27.12, where it clearly designates a horse (probably the usual means of conveyance for the Helfta nuns). It is used here as a metaphor of the divine heart.

11. *per tenuissimas rimas:* compare III.17.2, *quasi tenuis quaedam rima.*

12. Compare *Vere partum salutarem / in quo mater matrem parem / nullam habet precedentem / nec habebit subsequentem*: "A truly saving birth, in which the mother has no mother her equal, either preceding or following her": antiphon for various feasts of the Virgin.

they entrusted their loneliness to her motherly affections with the response, "Arise, virgin,"[13] intoned by
<Gertrud>, who was privileged to take a more intimate
part in <the abbess's> gladness. And so that virginal
body, the reverend temple of Christ Jesus, was carried
to the chapel by virgin hands and laid before the altar.
When the whole community had prostrated themselves
simultaneously around the body to pray, her soul appeared with unbelievable glory and honor, standing in
the presence of the ever-worshipful Trinity, praying for
all those who had formerly been entrusted to her.

25. While Mass was being sung for her, and <Gertrud>
was sorrowfully pondering her loneliness before the Lord,
gently comforting her he gave this reply: "Am I not sufficient compensation in her place for whatever I have taken
away from you all? On earth an honest man is trusted
if he appropriates the possessions of his dead knights,
because he will not allow their sons to perish; therefore
you should all trust even more in me, for I am Goodness
itself, because if *you are converted to me with all your*
heart,* for you I will myself be all that any of you mourn
having lost in her." And so from that moment when, as
said above, the Lord received that blessed soul, the heart
of Jesus dissolved over the whole world in such honeyed
loving-kindness that she who was permitted to perceive
this in spirit knew with the greatest certainty that there
was no righteous request made far and wide in the world
at that time that was not granted.

26. Then on the following day, on which the body
was to be buried, during the offertory of first Mass the
servant of God presented for that soul, to compensate
for her lack of merit, the most loving heart of Jesus

*Joel 2:12

---

13. Response for the feast of Saint Catherine of Alexandria.

Christ, just as he was able to possess it in union with his human nature, complete and perfect in all good things that had ever flowed from that heart into some human heart and had deliberately and unfailingly returned to it once more. When she was doing this, the Lord appeared to accept this in the likeness of a vessel in the shape of a human heart, which was filled with various delightful and precious presents. And when he had placed this in his bosom, he called the soul of our kindly mother to him with these words, "Come to me, little virgin, and distribute your possessions, which your daughters have sent you." At this she seemed to take up her position facing her beloved and, stretching out her hand towards the Lord's bosom, to consider carefully what lay within.

And when she found in that most worthy heart perfection of all virtues and all good things, with that loving affection that she had received from God by nature, lifting with her hand every single thing that she found, at each one she said, "Ah, my most loving Lord, this one would be right for the prioress and this one for her, and this one for her!" according to what she knew of each one's need on earth, which she longed to fill from the abundance of the virtues of the divine heart. At this the Lord, gazing lovingly at her, addressed her kindly, saying, "Come close, my chosen one." Then hastily getting up, she walked to the Lord's left side, and the Lord, raising his arm, embraced her and pressed her most delicately to his heart, saying, "Now see as I see." By this means she was allowed to perceive that it was human affection that had earlier induced her to share those gifts of virtues with her friends according to her knowledge on earth of their needs. But through that embrace God had so united her to himself that she could not will other than as God willed. And although he loves every person beyond human comprehension, he nonetheless allows some failings to persist in them by his divine dispensation.

27. Thence at the time of the elevation of the sacred Host, with it <Gertrud> offered God, for her dead mother's reward, the filial love that the heart of Jesus Christ felt for his own sweetest mother, Mary ever virgin. While she was doing this, the Son of God said most gently to that soul, "Come, little virgin, for I must show you the filial affection of my sweetest heart." Then the Blessed Virgin Mother Mary, gathering that soul into her embrace, led her to the Lord. The Lord Jesus leaned towards her and bestowed on her a most surpassingly delightful kiss, with which he gave her a certain foretaste of his filial affection. When this happened again and again at several Masses, at length, when a good twenty or more had been sung, <Gertrud> was longing to offer something more to the increase of her dearest mother's merits. So she also offered that filial affection that Christ Jesus had to God the Father in his divine nature, and to Mary his mother in his human nature. While she was doing this, rising up, the Son of God stood before the Father and summoned the dead woman's soul, saying, "Come here, lady queen, for now you have been sent something greater!" And when she, conducted by the mother of the Lord, was once more raised up greatly on high, she who saw this said to her, "Now I can no longer see you, lady mother, nor can I perceive anything further about your rewards." And she replied, "But you could certainly question me about what you wish to learn."

28. Then she said, "Good mother, why do your prayers not win from God the ability for us to restrain our tears? For we are pouring forth our tears so copiously for your loss that we are harming our heads, although it often irked you when we distorted our features for no good reason." She replied, "My Lord, who loves

me tenderly, grants me for glory and profit that in which others have little profit. For in return for that discretion with which I sought to rule you so discreetly, he has now allowed me to offer all your tears to my Lord, as if in a golden cup. From its overflow in return for each tear he pours out a little stream of his own honey-sweet divine nature for me; joyfully drinking from that, I sing songs of thanksgiving to my beloved for my daughters and for all those who wept."

29. And when she asked whether this happened only from those tears that were shed for God's honor, because people feared damage to the religious life from her death, she replied, "This applies to all tears, including those shed solely from affection, but as for those that flow for God's honor, as you said, in return for them the Son of God himself sings with me in thanksgiving. And I find this as much the more delightful as the Creator is removed from his creatures." Then, addressing her by name, she said, "Concerning you, my daughter, I have received a special reward from God, because, as you know, I encouraged you faithfully and lovingly in that particular matter,[14] to God's praise. For in the heart of my beloved Lord Jesus, like a sweet-sounding pipe, is sung to me an unceasing love song,[15] for which all the court of heaven glorifies me. And in addition to this sweetest sound, my eyes are granted most delightful splendor, and my nostrils and mouth sweetest smell and taste. But no special pleasure is granted my sense of touch because I was slightly negligent there, although with good intentions and for the sake of peace."

14. *in illa causa*: this must refer to the abbess's command to Gertrud to have her revelations recorded in writing.

15. *layum amoris*, the only occurrence of this phrase in LDP.

30. And when the bell was being struck at the elevation of the Host, <Gertrud> offered God that Host in compensation for that dead woman's failings. While she was doing this, the Host that was being offered appeared before the dead woman in the shape of a most delectable scepter, which seemed to dance around in a most delightful way. But she herself could never touch this scepter, for whatever we fail to do here can never be entirely made good in the next life. From the grateful loving-kindness that she had received from God, she seemed to pray for all those who had gathered together to celebrate her funeral rites, so that through her merits each one was granted remission of very many sins, and from divine grace the strength to do well was increased.

31. At the blessing that ended one of the Masses, our blessed mother appeared, standing before the throne of the worshipful Trinity and asking, "O giver of gifts, by the gift of your loving-kindness grant this grace to my dead bones, that as often as my daughters come to my tomb and lament their loneliness or their failings, they may remember through the experience of consolation in some way that I am their mother." God, most kind, lovingly assented to these words and from his divine omnipotence, wisdom, and kindliness gave an individual blessing to each. Now when that happy and truly blessed mother was placed in the tomb, the Lord seemed to make the sign of the cross over the body with outstretched hand every time some earth was thrown on her reverend body, to confirm that blessing. But the last time, when all the earth had been heaped up, the Virgin Mary, mother of the Lord, also made the sign of the cross above the tomb with her delicate hand, as if impressing a seal, in witness that the Lord had bestowed such a gift on the dead woman.

32. Then after the burial, while they were intoning the response, "The kingdom of the world,"[16] such
great glory and exultation appeared in heaven as if all
the stones in a single building, of both the walls and
the floor, were being moved by a special exultation.
Meanwhile, there appeared a choir of most beautiful
virgins, preceded by that woman whose funeral was
taking place, as if she were Queen of virgins, bearing
in her hand with a most delicate gesture a pure white
lily with springtime loveliness of various flowers. With
the other hand she was leading those virgins after her,
of whom the closest were those of the community who
had been in her charge and had already been glorified.
After them followed the other heavenly virgins.

33. And when they had arrived in this way before the
throne of God with glory and indescribable exultation,
at the phrase "whom I have seen,"[17] <Gertrud> saw God
the Father bestowing new gifts on this woman who was
going on ahead. Also at the phrase "whom I have loved,"
she saw the Son of God similarly bestow gifts on her,
and the Holy Spirit at that phrase "in whom I have believed." But at that phrase "whom I have adored," she
saw the dead woman stretch out her delicate arms and
tenderly embrace Jesus, her most loving spouse. After
this, while they were singing the response, "Free me,

16. *Regnum mundi et omnem ornatum saeculi contempsi prop-
ter amorem domini mei Jesu Christi, quem vidi, quem amavi, in
quem credidi, quem dilexi,* "The kingdom of this world and all
worldly adornment have I despised for the love of my lord Jesus
Christ, whom I have seen, whom I have loved, in whom I have
believed, whom I have esteemed": response from the Common
of Virgins. See also IV.54.3.

17. See previous note.

Lord,"[18] she saw another choir in heaven, in which were rejoicing those souls that had reached heaven on that very day through the Masses and prayers offered for her and also through her merits. Among them she noticed in particular that the soul of a laybrother in the monastery, who was judged to have been somewhat negligent in spiritual things, had been greatly comforted through the merits of that person, that is, of our glorious mother.

34. On her month's mind[19] our renowned and blessed mother appeared once again, adorned with such wonderful-colored clothing that whatever had been shown earlier paled into insignificance. In her shone forth every reward that she had received from God's loving-kindness because she was burdened in this life by corporeality.[20] There also appeared before the throne a golden book, wonderfully decorated, in which seemed to be inscribed all the teaching she had given her subjects on earth, and whenever someone acted on her words or examples it was still being recorded, for her reward.

35. And when she who saw these things[21] asked what special reward she had for her right hand, in which <the abbess> had suffered great pain, she replied, "With it I sweetly embrace my beloved, and my heart's inestimable joy is this, that Jesus himself, most loving, deigns to wear it like a collar, and delights to enjoy it as a sweet embrace." For all her right side, from head to

18. *Libera me, domine, de morte aeterna in die illa tremenda quando caeli movendi sunt et terra,* "Deliver me, Lord, from eternal death on that fearful day when the heavens and earth shall be moved": response for the Office of the Dead.

19. Mass celebrated thirty days (i.e. about a month) after a person's death.

20. *corpulentia*, which can also mean "obesity," but that seems unlikely in context.

21. See p. xxx.

toe, was adorned as if with gems of wonderful beauty, and it reflected that same beauty onto the left side. For the right side that was adorned symbolized the reward she had received for that sickness, and the beauty on the left symbolized the reward that she had received because her will worked in harmony with God's. And so from one part to another rays were being transmitted, dancing to and fro just as the sun dances on water. In return for her loss of speech, as soon as she had died she received such a kiss from the Lord that she will keep for ever that splendor issuing from a mouth so beautiful that from it all the court of heaven take special joy.

36. During the Mass <Gertrud> was wholeheartedly beseeching the Lord that he would restore to "the soul of my mother and Lady Abbess," so often mentioned, whatever benefit he had bestowed upon her. The Lord said, "Yes: any of you might help me, because right now I cannot refuse to pour any good thing in its entirety into that soul." Then, gazing lovingly at the soul, he said, "Truly, what has been paid back with such gratitude has been well paid out!" Then that woman, proceeding before the throne of glory, gave thanks to God for the loyalty of those subject to her in these words: "Eternal praise, vast and unchanging, be to you, my sweetest God, for all your benefits, and blessed be that time in which you prepared me to receive such salutary and most delicious fruit." And she added, "Ah, God of my life, *answer* them *for me*."* The Lord replied, "*I will fix the eyes* of my mercy *upon* them."* And thus the Lord appeared to make two signs of the cross with his most holy hand, with which he gave each member of the community grace to provide a good example outwardly in deed, and increase of divine love inwardly in the heart.

*see Isa 38:14

*see Ps 31:8

CHAPTER TWO

THE SOUL OF E., COMPARED
TO A LILY BY THE LORD

1. Now on the twelfth day after the death of Lady
G\<ertrud> of blessed memory, our most kindly abbess,
another person, one of her bereaved daughters, also died.
Her passing piled *sorrow above sorrow** on the community, for she had been much *beloved of God and men* and
women,* both for the glory of her most innocent purity
and great devotion and for the wonderful charm of her
character and her friendliness towards all. After her death,
recalling the charm of her company, moved by sorrow,
\<Gertrud> said to the Lord, "Ah, most loving Lord, why
did you take her away from us so suddenly?" The Lord
replied, "While you were conducting the funeral rites of
my beloved G\<ertrud> the abbess, delighting in the community's most attentive devotion I came down, as it were,
to feed among the lilies.* And when I saw that lily that
greatly pleased my sight, I laid my hand on it! And while
I held it for eleven days between my fingers preparing to
pick it, developing a wonderful scent and beauty, it grew
stronger and stronger from that very sickness. So now I
have taken it for myself and delight in it." And the Lord
added, "Whenever any of you, remembering the charm
of her company, longs to have her still, if she then offers
her up to my will, she holds before my nostrils a most
delightfully scented lily, which I shall repay a hundredfold, according to my loving-kindness."

*see Jer 8:18

*see Sir 45:1

*see
Song 2:16

29

2. And when at the elevation of the Host, she was offering the faithfulness of the heart of Jesus for her with sisterly faithfulness, she saw her raised to greater dignity, as if she were being placed in higher dignity and dressed in more resplendent garments and honored by more glorious servants. And she saw this as often as she made the same offering for her. Hence when she asked the Lord how it had come about that this same virgin, while she was dying, had both appeared and sounded terrified, she received this answer: "My overwhelming faithfulness inflicted this on her. For since a few days before that sickness she had desired to obtain through your prayers that I would receive her after death without any obstacle, and receiving my assurance from you, she faithfully believed it; considering her trust I was pleased to bless her greatly. And since it is rare for youth to be completely purified from less serious sins, such as taking pleasure in what is not strictly necessary and the like, and she had to be purified from such sins through the sorrow of sickness, although I was already calling her to glory, I allowed such sorrow, so patiently endured, fully to grant her eternal glory. And so I permitted her to be terrified by the appearance of a demon, so that this might act as complete purification for her, and all the other things by which she had been purified would render her eternal reward." Then she said, "Where were you, hope of the hopeless,[1] during this?" The Lord replied, "I had concealed myself on her left, but as soon as she was purified, I presented myself to her and took her up with me to rest and eternal glory."

---

1. Innocent III, *De sacro altaris mysterio / De missarum mysteriis* II.45 (PL 217:825).

CHAPTER THREE

THE SOUL OF G., WHO WAS
DEVOTED TO THE BLESSED VIRGIN

1. After this, a girl passed away who had been specially devoted to the Mother of our Savior from her childhood. Having completed her earthly race, she was called *to the prize of the supernal** reward. Most devoutly prepared by all the sacraments of the church, on her deathbed she took the image of the Crucified in her hands, which were already nearly dead, and greeted the holy wounds with honeyed words, gave thanks, worshiped, and pressed sweetest kisses on each one, so that she wonderfully inspired those who were present to compunction. And afterwards, when with various short prayers she had requested forgiveness of sins, restitution for her failings, and safe passage from the Lord, the most blessed Virgin Mary, the holy angels, and all the saints, she finally rested very briefly as if weary and fell asleep blessedly in the Lord. And when the community had devoted itself to prayer for the relief of her soul, the Lord Jesus appeared to <Gertrud>, holding the dead girl's soul in his arms. Caressingly he held her chin and said to her, "Do you recognize me, my daughter?" And when she who saw these things was praying the Lord to give her a special reward for that humility with which she had willingly served her and other women too who <Gertrud> believed were greatly pleasing to God, that she might share in their grace, the Lord offered that dead

*see Phil 3:14

31

girl his deified heart with these words, "Now drink from a cup, filled to the brim, what you thirsted for from me through my chosen."[1]

2. Now the next day, during Mass, the soul of the dead girl appeared as if sitting on the Lord's lap. And the Queen of Heaven, that is, the Mother of the Lord, seemed to be there too, offering her own joys and merits to her. And in particular while the community was reciting the Psalter for her with an *Ave* after each psalm,[2] while the community was reciting them, at every word the Mother of Mercy seemed to offer that soul presents, which she accepted as if to increase her reward. Then <Gertrud>, longing to know, asked the Lord what stain the soul of that dead girl had incurred from human weakness that he had judged should particularly be purified in her before she left the body. The Lord replied, "She was a little too attached to her own opinion. I purified this in her, in that she died before the community had completed its collective prayer for her. She was extremely anxious, because she was afraid this would do her great harm, since she saw that the community's prayers were unfinished. And this purified her from that failing."

3. And while she was saying, "Lord, could this not have been purified through contrition of heart, when she sought forgiveness of all her sins from you in her passing?" the Lord replied, "It could not be purified through such general contrition because she persisted in her own opinion a little too much, not fully submitting to those

---

1. *Liber carnis vinculo / caelum introivit / ubi pleno poculo / gustat quod sitivit*, "Released from the bonds of the flesh he entered heaven, where from a cup, filled to the brim, he tasted what he thirsted for": antiphon for the feast of Saint Dominic.

2. See the description in V.18.1 of the recitation for the dead of the Great Psalter.

who were instructing her. And thus she had to be purified by suffering." And the Lord added, "There was still another reason that she had to be purified: she was reluctant to go to confession. But my loving-kindness released her because of the presence of my friends and hers, who cared for her, and I forgave her all the guilt that she had incurred in that respect, requiring only the suffering that forced her to confess on the day of her death."

4. During Mass, while they were chanting "<We offer to thee, O Lord,> sacrifice and prayers"[3] at the Offertory, the Lord seemed to raise his right hand, and from it emanated a wonderful brightness that as it were lit up the whole sky. In particular that soul, which appeared sitting on the Lord's lap, was wonderfully illuminated. All the saints, coming forward according to their choirs' rank, offered their own rewards to Christ Jesus' lap, to supplement the rewards of that soul. And she understood that this happened because while that soul was still alive in the body, she was accustomed to pray that this should happen for the salvation of the souls of the dead.[4] Although all the saints showed themselves so friendly towards her, in particular her fellow virgins encouraged her with most sweet support.

5. Another time, when <Gertrud> was praying for her with few but weighty words, all those words that she had spoken in prayer appeared as if written on Jesus' breast and forming windows, as it were, that opened onto the heart of Jesus, the Son of God. And she heard the Lord saying to that soul, "Look all around heaven,

---

3. *Hostias et preces tibi, domine, offerimus,* "Lord, we offer you prayers and sacrifices": the words of the priest over the elements at the Offertory of a requiem Mass.

4. She probably used the prayer, "Grant them, O Lord, eternal rest, and may light perpetual shine upon them."

and consider whether you can see something in any of the saints that you would like to have, and draw it from my heart through those windows." She perceived that the same thing happened with every prayer that was devoutly recited for her.

6. Now at the elevation of the Host, the Son of God seemed to offer that soul his body in the form of a spotless little lamb; when she bestowed a most sweet kiss on it, she seemed to be transformed in that kiss as if she had received new joy in knowledge of the Godhead. Then <Gertrud> asked her to pray for those entrusted to her. She replied, "I do pray for them, but I can only will what I see to be willed by my most loving Lord." Then <Gertrud> said, "Does it do them no good to hope in your prayer?" She replied, "It does a great deal of good, for when the Lord sees their desire, he inspires us to pray for them." <Gertrud> replied, "Can one pray more specially for your special friends who have not requested it?" She said, "Our Lord benefits them greatly for our sake from his natural loving-kindness." Then <Gertrud> asked, "Please pray more specially for that priest who at this moment is receiving communion for you." She replied, "He will receive double profit from it, for just as the Lord receives it from him and returns it to me as salvation, so it is returned from me to him after I too have been enhanced by it, just as gold appears more lovely when set off by different colors." Then <Gertrud> said, "You seem to assert by what you say that it is more profitable to celebrate Mass for the dead than for anyone else." She replied, "His helping souls because of charity is more profitable than if he were celebrating another Mass only because it is his priestly duty. But it is most profitable if he is borne towards God by the arousal of his heart, and thus celebrates." And when <Gertrud> said to her, "How do you know all this, although when

you were alive your intelligence was rather modest?" she replied, "I have it from the source of which Augustine says, 'Once to have gazed into him, is to have learned all things.'"

7. Another time, seeing her in great glory, dressed in red garments, she asked the Lord why she had these. The Lord replied, "As I had promised her through you, I have vested her in my passion, because although she suffered from a serious heart defect she did not withdraw from the communal labors of the Order. And when she labored beyond her strength in such activities, she nonetheless did not complain loudly and impatiently." And the Lord added, "Also because she endured some inadequate care in her sickness, I granted her many servants from my more noble princes, who frequently provide her with special and glorious delight in return for each of those inadequacies that she endured. And because she suffered rather severe pain in one arm, she embraces me with such blessed glory that she would have chosen to suffer a hundred times more."

8. Then <Gertrud> saw certain souls seated in very great glory coming to kneel before her: they had been released through prayers that had been offered for her but were more than she needed. And when <Gertrud> asked her if the community was helped by very many of its members having already been received into heaven, she replied, "It is indeed a great support for you, for the Lord multiplies his blessings towards you because of each one." And when <Gertrud> was praying for her during another Mass, which was not being sung for the dead, seeing her in glory she asked her what benefit she could have from that Mass, as it was not being sung for the dead. She replied, "And what benefit does a queen have from the possessions of her lord king? For now that I am united with the King, my Lord and sweetest

spouse, in truth I share all his possessions, just as a queen shares the king's table." For this be praise and glory for ever and ever to the Lord, the King of kings!

CHAPTER FOUR

THE BLESSED DEATH
OF MECHTILD THE CHANTRESS
OF PIOUS MEMORY[1]

1. When Lady Mechtild of blessed memory, our most devoted chantress, was sick unto death, full of good works and of God, scarcely a month before her decease and already bedridden, with her customary devotion and virtuous will she eagerly studied the exercise in preparation for death that <Gertrud> had composed. On the Sunday on which, through reception of the most holy Body and Blood, she was committing her final moments to the divine mercy, while praying for her <Gertrud> realized in spirit that by his divine power the Lord had completely breathed in her soul and after a while had breathed it back again into her dear body, to remain there for a time. Then she said to the Lord, "Why, Lord, do you still want her to linger on earth?" "So that I may perfect the work that by my divine dispensation I have pre-ordained to be done in these days. And to this end she will provide me with threefold service, that is, the repose of humility, the banquet of patience, and the entertainment of virtues. That is, she will always look upon herself with humility in all that she sees or hears

---

1. Mechtild died on November 19, 1298, seven years after her sister the Abbess Gertrud.

*RB 7.51

*RB 7.39

from anyone, and will consider herself *unworthy and more worthless than everyone*;* through this she will provide me with sufficiently delightful repose in her heart and soul. Second, *rejoicing** in all her infirmities and tribulations, she is embracing patience and will freely endure all burdens for my love, and in this way she prepares a truly sumptuous banquet for me. Third, through the practice of various virtues she provides my divine pleasure with most delightful entertainment."[2]

2. Another time when about to communicate, she was asking the Lord what he was about in <Mechtild>; he replied, "I am reposing in the marriage-chamber of her sweet embrace." In these words she understood that "the marriage-chamber of her sweet embrace," in which she reposed with the Lord, and the Lord with her, was this: although she was troubled by various burdens and continual pains, nonetheless trusting in the Lord's loving-kindness she believed that everything happened to her for her salvation from the divine mercy, and she always gave thanks to God, faithfully entrusting all things to his fatherly providence.

3. Since she was by now hastening towards death, and was tortured every evening by an unbearable pain in her heart, on one occasion she kindly comforted her sisters, who were standing around and sharing her most bitter pains, saying, "Ah, *do not weep* or sorrow *over me,** dearest ones, for I feel your desolation so greatly that if it were the will of our sweetest lover, I would be willing to live in this pain for ever so that I could comfort you in all things." On one occasion when she was pressed more urgently by the prayers of some of the women to take medicine that would, they hoped,

*see
Luke 23:28

2. For this metaphor of the lordly banquet followed by the entertainment or diversion provided by a minstrel, see also IV.54.1.

dull the pain, and although unwilling she nonetheless graciously agreed, after she had taken the medicine she experienced more acute pain. The next day when <Gertrud> was asking the Lord how he would recompense the sick woman for such graciousness, the Lord replied, "From that pain that my beloved incurred in the evening, when she graciously accepted medicine at the prayers of others, I have compounded a most effective remedy for all sinners throughout the whole world and for all souls that require purification."

4. On the second-last Sunday [of the liturgical year], that is, *If <you, O Lord, will mark> iniquities,**³   *Ps 129:3 Mechtild received communion for the last time before her death. The Lord inspired <Gertrud>, who was praying for her, to warn his chosen one to prepare to receive the sacrament of the anointing of the sick. For her own part, she was to tell her that after the reception of that life-giving sacrament the most attentive Guardian of his friends would himself guard her in his bosom from every spot, as a painter guards the picture he has just painted with the greatest care, lest it should be obscured by dust. She told the sick woman this, but she did not herself want to do anything to forward matters, as she was always subject to her superiors in all things, humbly submitting to their decree. Instead she completely entrusted herself to Divine Providence, who has never abandoned those whose hope is in him. But her superiors held her in such great regard that they were quite sure she would certainly know in advance the time that the Lord would wish <Mechtild> to receive this sacrament, so when they saw that she was not earnestly requesting this, they put off the sacrament of anointing on that day.

3. Introit for the twenty-second Sunday after Pentecost.

But the Lord, validating that verse from the gospel, *Heaven and earth shall pass, but my words shall not pass,** demonstrated the truth of the word that he had spoken to his chosen one by this proof: before Matins on the Monday, blessed M<echtild> of happy memory began to be so afflicted by sudden pains that she was most certainly thought to be dying. Priests were then hastily summoned, she received the sacrament of the anointing of the sick, and so it happened that she was anointed, although not on that very day,[4] nonetheless before dawn on the next day.

*Matt 24:35

5. While <Gertrud> was praying for her, she perceived that while the sick woman's eyes were being anointed by the priest, with a ray of divine splendor the most loving Lord turned towards her most graciously the full gaze of his divine loving-kindness, which constantly moves his heart, flowing with honey, in its own goodness. With that splendor he gave her the use of his own most holy eyes. Then she saw Mechtild's eyes exude, as it were, a liquid of sweetest oil out of the abundance of the divine loving-kindness. She perceived from this that through her merits the Lord was generously condescending to bestow the succor of consolation on all those invoking her with confidence. And she earned this privilege because she always showed herself kind and well-disposed towards everyone, with loving charity. In the same way, when the other limbs[5] were being anointed, at each one the Lord granted her most complete use of his own most holy limbs. But at the anointing of her mouth,[6] uncontrollably zealous for her

---

4. That is, the Sunday.
5. In the Middle Ages, seven parts of the body were anointed.
6. Possibly because Mechtild had been the chantress.

soul, he most graciously prepared to offer his spouse a kiss on the mouth, surpassing a draught of honey;[7] with this he bestowed on her all the fruitfulness of his most holy mouth.

6. When they were reciting in the Litany, "All you holy seraphim and cherubim, pray for her," she saw that, with the deepest reverence and greatest dance of exultation, those blessed seraphim and cherubim, moving away from one other, had offered God's chosen one a most suitable seat among themselves. They considered that on earth she had led the life of an angel through the holiness of her virginity, and, even more than the angels, with the cherubim had drunk copiously streams of spiritual understanding from the very fount of all wisdom, and with the fiery seraphim had embraced the one who is *a consuming fire.** She therefore should be placed among them on high, as they deserved above all others to be near the divine majesty. And when the saints were named in the Litany, each of them rose up with immense joy and the greatest reverence, and kneeling, presented their merits to the Lord's bosom in the form of precious gifts, to increase the joy and glory of his beloved. When the anointing was finished, the Lord embraced her most lovingly and supported her for two days so that the wound of his sweetest heart lay open at the sick woman's mouth. Every breath that she drew, she seemed to breathe in from there, and to breathe out again into the sweetest heart.

*Deut 4:24

7. Now the most joyful time of her blessed passing was approaching, at which, after the distress of various sicknesses, the Lord had determined to give his chosen one the uninterrupted sleep of eternal rest. On the

---

7. See also IV.5.1, lines 16–19.

Tuesday, that is, the vigil of the feast of Saint Elizabeth,[8] it was obvious before None that she was beginning her death agony. The community had gathered with great devotion and, in expectation of the death of their sister in Christ, so dear to them, were fortifying her with the customary prayers. <Gertrud>, led by more burning desire, saw her soul in the form of a most delicate young girl standing before the Lord and breathing out every breath that she breathed in through the wound in the most holy side, into that heart that was flowing with honey. As a result, as often as the deified heart, moved by the unrestraint of its own kindness and sweetness, drew in her breath, it overflowed from superabundance of love and sprinkled showers of grace throughout the breadth of the Church, and specially on those there present. She perceived that this was because at that moment, thanks to God's gift, that blessed invalid had a specially devout intention and fervent desire for all those, both living and dead, to whom the Lord generously dispensed his gifts of grace.

8. While they were reciting the antiphon "Hail, queen," at that phrase, "Ah, therefore, our advocate," the sick woman, God's chosen one, lovingly addressed the Virgin Mother and entrusted to her the companions whom she was close to leaving. She prayed that she would receive them with greater love and that just as she had offered herself while alive to them all, as far as she could, as a benevolent and willing advocate, so the Mother of Mercy herself would now, after her death, condescend to be mediator and advocate of the community with her before her Son. The spotless Virgin showed herself most willing to do this and, stretching

---

8. At that time the feast of Saint Elizabeth of Hungary was celebrated on November 19. The vigil, November 18, fell on a Tuesday in 1298.

out her delicate hands to the hands of the sick woman, accepted the care of the community entrusted to her as if from her hand. Then while they were reciting the short prayer, "Hail, Jesu Christ," at this phrase, "sweet way," the Lord Jesus, tender spouse of her soul, appeared, as if smoothing the way for his bride with the oil[9] of his divine nature, that he might draw her to him more sweetly and tenderly.

9. And in this way she lay dying all day and said nothing except "Good Jesu! good Jesu!" showing most openly that deep in her heart was fixed the one whose name, in the midst of the bitter pains of death, she constantly ruminated in her mouth. And when they one by one devoutly entrusted themselves to her prayers and commended to her whatever their needs might be, she would at least murmur "Gladly," or "Yes," even though she could Bernard, not say any more. She expressly declared by this the love with which she was commending to the Lord whatever had been entrusted to her. <Gertrud> perceived that from all the limbs in which the sick woman was suffering there issued, as it were, an extraordinary exhalation that, as it touched her soul, purified it miraculously from all spot of sin, sanctified her, and made her fit for eternal blessedness.

10. Although she had learned all this in spirit, she decided in her heart that she would keep all these things hidden, lest she should be known as the one to whom it was revealed. But what followed made abundantly clear that this was against the wishes of the Lord, *whose glory is to search the speech** and who said, *That which you hear in the ear, preach upon the housetops.*† For during the vespers of Saint Elizabeth, it once again seemed to

*Bernard, SC 65.2, and see Prov 25:2

†Matt 3:27

9. *adipe*, literally "fat."

be so obvious that Lady M<echtild> was dying that the
community was quickly summoned from choir and was
repeating the customary prayers over the sick woman.
But however strongly she exerted her inner senses,
<Gertrud> could not perceive a single thing of what was
happening to the sick woman until she acknowledged
her guilt and, washing it away by repenting, promised
the Lord that she would willingly make known whatever
he deigned to reveal to her, to his glory alone and for
the consolation of her neighbors.

11. Then after Compline, while that sick woman was
now in her death agony for the third time, again caught
up in spirit <Gertrud> saw the sick woman's soul, as
before, in the form of a very tender and lovable little
girl, but as it were made lovely with new adornments
and lengthy sufferings, rushing impetuously to the neck
of Jesus Christ, her delicate spouse, and holding him
with charming embraces. Like a bee busily sucking all
kinds of flowers, she drew into herself special pleasures
from each of the Lord's wounds. When they were reciting, among others, the responsory "Hail spouse, Queen
of virgins, rose without thorn,"[10] <the Virgin> came
forward and rendered her fit to enjoy and take pleasure
in divine delights. Then from his Mother's merits and
from that dignity by which she alone deserved to be
called Mother and Virgin (as she is indeed), the Lord
Jesus took, as it were, a necklace made of wonderfully
glittering gems. He placed it on the sick woman's breast,
at the same time endowing her with the special privilege
that she too should be called mother and virgin like his
own Virgin Mother because she had given birth with
chaste zeal to mindfulness of him in the hearts of many.

---

10. *Ave sponsa, virginum regina, rosa sine spina*: unidentified.

12. And so on the night of the feast of Saint Elizabeth, when Matins had already started, God's chosen one once again showed such changes that it was thought that she was breathing her last. So, abandoning Matins, the community quickly gathered around her in the customary way. Then, shining in the splendor of his divine strength, the Lord appeared dressed like a bridegroom, *crowned with glory and honor** and miraculously   *see Ps 8:6 adorned by the beauty of his indescribably dazzling divine nature. Then, addressing the sick woman's soul with sweetest caress, he said, "Soon, my beloved, I *shall exalt you among your neighbors,** that is, in the   *Sir 15:4 presence of the community so dear to me." And thus in a way beyond understanding or thought he greeted that most blessed soul through each of the wounds of his most holy body, and indeed each wound emitted four wonderful manners of invitation, filled with all delight: that is, a most delightful sound, a most potent exhalation, a most abundant dew, and a most lovely splendor. Through these the Lord greeted his chosen one and summoned her as she was about to die.

13. The sweet sound, which surpassed every kind of musical instrument, symbolized all the words that God's chosen one had spoken, either sweetly to God or profitably for God, throughout her life for the salvation of her neighbors. All these, made sweet a hundredfold in the divine heart, were rewarded by the emissions of each of the Lord's wounds. The truly wonderful exhalation symbolized all the desires that she had had for God's praise, or for God's sake for the salvation of all. These too were repaid her, multiplied by a power beyond human understanding, through each of Jesus' sweet-flowing wounds. The generous dew expressed every feeling of love that she had ever felt for God, or for another creature for God's sake, which also affected her soul with

indescribably sweet-flowing delight through the Lord's wounds. The dazzling splendor symbolized the various physical and spiritual sufferings that she had endured from childhood until the present, which, having been ennobled beyond all human capacity in union with the sufferings of Jesus, sanctified her soul and made it fit for divine brightness.

14. Resting in the enjoyment of heavenly delights, that soul did not expire at that moment but still aspired to the loftier good things to be made ready for her by her lover. Copiously sprinkling those present with the generous dew of his divine blessing, the Lord said, "Compelled by my own goodness, I was delighting inwardly in the sweetness of love that all the members of this community, so dear to me, should be present at this transfiguration of my most worthy <beloved>. From this may they have honor in heaven in the presence of all my saints as great as those three, chosen above all, that is Peter, James, and John, have above the other apostles, because they were worthy to be present at my transfiguration on the mountain." Then she asked, "Lord, what good can your generous blessing and copious infusion of graces do those who do not taste this inwardly?" The Lord replied, "When someone is given a fruitful orchard by his lord, he cannot taste each fruit at once, but he must wait until the fruit ripens. In the same way when I grant someone gifts of grace, they do not immediately experience the taste of inner pleasure until through the practice of exterior virtues, having completely shattered the outer shell of earthly pleasures, they deserve to relish the kernel of inner delight." Then having received a most salutary blessing, the community once again re-entered the choir and finished Matins.

15. While they were chanting the twelfth response, "O lamp,"[11] the sick woman's soul appeared, standing in the sight of the supreme Trinity, devoutly praying for the church. Sweetly chanting the same words, God the Father greeted her, saying, "Hail, my chosen one, for through the example of your holy life you could rightly be called *lamp of the church, pouring out rivers of oil,* that is, of prayers, throughout the length and breadth of the world." Then God the Son added, "Rejoice, my spouse, you are rightly called *medicine of grace,* for by your prayers grace is restored more abundantly to the various people who lack it." Then the Holy Spirit sang, 'Hail, my spotless one, who will deservedly be called *nourishment of faith*, for in all hearts that piously believe in my divine work that I am working in you, not physically but spiritually, the virtue of faith is nourished and strengthened."

16. Then God the Father granted her that from his omnipotence she might provide protection to all those *trembling* from human weakness and not yet fully confident in the divine goodness. Also the Holy Spirit bestowed on her that out of the fervor of his own divine love she might offer warmth to the lukewarm. Then the Son of God granted her that in union with his most holy passion and death she might bestow *healing* on all those *languishing* in sin. Then a multitude of angels and saints, lifting her up before the Lord with honor, made resound together with clear voice, "You are the

---

11. *O lampas ecclesiae, / rivos fundens olei, / medicina gratiae / nutrimentum fidei / tutelam presta pavidis / calorem minus fervidis / languidis medelam,"* "O lamp of the church, / pouring out rivers of oil, / medicine of grace, / nourishment of faith, / provide protection to the trembling, / warmth to the lukewarm / healing to the sick": response for the feast of Saint Elizabeth of Hungary from the hymn *Laetare Germania.*

abundance of God, a fruitful olive, whose purity illuminates, and whose works shine forth";[12] with that phrase
whose purity illuminates, they praised in consort the
most delightful repose with which the Lord worthily
reposed in her soul, and with that phrase *her works shine
forth*, the praiseworthy and single-minded intention of
all her works. Then all the saints intoned with high voice
the antiphon "God openly revealing <his righteous sal-
vation> to all <peoples>" and so on.[13]

17. During the preface at High Mass, as if endued
with a new and glorious beauty, Jesus, the vigorous
bridegroom, once again turned his spouse's face with
sweetest caress so exactly opposite his own face that he
seemed to draw in direct the sick woman's breath by his
own breathing. Placing his own deified eyes opposite
her eyes,[14] he wonderfully gazed upon her and, blessedly sanctifying her, fitted her for the glory of future
blessedness.

18. Then that most desirable hour was at hand, at
which the chosen spouse of Christ Jesus, perfectly prepared according to the most excellent pleasure of her
beloved, was about to enter the bridegroom's marriage
chamber. The Lord of majesty himself, *flowing with de-*
*Song 8:5   lights,** encircling her completely with the light of his
divine nature, was intoning most sweetly, *Come, you
*Matt 25:34   blessed of my Father, possess the kingdom,** and *Arise,
*see   make haste, my love, and come,** reminding her of that
Song 2:10

12. *Tu Dei saturitas, oliva fructifera, cuius lucet puritas, et
resplendent opera*: from the response for the feast of Saint Elizabeth of Hungary (as above).
13. *Deus palam omnibus revelans justitiam salutarem gentibus
per hanc infudit gratiam*, "God openly revealing to all peoples
his righteous salvation infused grace through her": antiphon for
the feast of Saint Elizabeth of Hungary (as above).
14. Cf. II.21.1, lines 9–14.

most worthy gift when a few years before[15] he had given her his heart with the same words as a pledge of love, and of all the pleasures and consolations that he had continually offered her during the same time. Then, greeting her most caressingly, he said, "And where is my present?" After this, with both hands she opened her own heart directly opposite her beloved's heart, similarly opened opposite hers, and the Lord pressed his own most holy heart to hers and blessedly united her in her entirety, absorbed by the power of his divine nature, to his glory. There may she, mindful of those mindful of her, obtain for us, we pray, the grace of God's loving-kindness!

19. And then, when the commendation of the dead was being recited in the customary way, the Lord appeared seated in the majesty of his glory, gently caressing the dead woman's soul as it rested in his bosom. When they were reciting, "Come to her assistance, you saints of God; run to help her before the Lord, sustain her soul,"[16] the angels, seeing her welcomed with such great condescension by their Lord and honored so magnificently, knelt before the Lord like princes accepting estates from the emperor and received back their own merits, which they had offered the day before at the sacrament of anointing to increase the merit of Christ's beloved, as if they had been doubled by her merits and miraculously ennobled. Each of the saints did the same when their names were invoked in the Litany.

20. Then <Gertrud> reminded her in spirit that she should pray for the failings of her special friends. She replied, "I now see clearly in the light of truth that all

15. On the Wednesday following Easter: see *Special Grace* II.19.

16. *Subvenite sancti Dei, occurrite angeli Domini, suscipientes animam ejus:* response for the Office of the Dead.

the affection that I felt on earth for someone is scarcely, as it were, a single drop compared to the vast expanse of that ocean of sweetest love felt towards them by the divine heart. I also see by how useful a dispensation the Lord allows some failings to persist in a person, by which they are humbled and often distressed, and thus day by day he promotes their salvation. For even with a single thought I could not will anything other than what my Lord's all-powerful wisdom has decreed for each of these according to his good pleasure. So I exert myself completely in praise and thanksgiving for the disposition, so well ordered, of the divine loving-kindness."

21. The next day, during the first Mass, that is, "Rest eternal,"[17] God's chosen one appeared, putting forth as it were golden pipes from the heart of God for all those who had a special devotion to her, through which they could draw whatever they desired from the divine heart. Each pipe had a golden stopper,[18] which they had to extract to obtain whatever they desired by saying these or similar words: "Through the love by which you ever blessed your chosen M<echtild> or any of your chosen, or would have done had you found the potential in them, and will still do in heaven or on earth, hear me, most kindly Jesu, through her merits and those of all your chosen," trusting that through such words they could move the divine clemency to whatever was desired. Indeed, at the elevation of the Host, that blessed soul seemed to desire to be offered to God the Father together with the Host, to his eternal praise for the salvation of the whole world. Then God's Only-Begotten, who cannot deny the desire of his chosen, drew her in completely and, offering her to God the Father with

17. *Requiem eternam*, Mass for the dead.
18. See also LDP III.53.2.

himself, from that union granted an increase in salvation to all those in heaven and on earth and in purgatory.

22. Then another time, when she once again appeared in glory, <Gertrud> asked her what she had gained from her close friends' having recited to the Lord on her behalf the antiphon *From whom are all things*[19] as many times as the number of days she had lived on earth, and having had as many Masses of the Holy Trinity sung as the number of years she had lived, in praise, glory, and thanksgiving for all the benefits bestowed upon her. She replied, "In return for the antiphon *From whom are all things*, my Lord adorned me with as many lovely flowers as the antiphons they had recited; through those flowers I inhale living sweetness from his heart, flowing with honey. In return for the Masses, he has granted me that in all the praise with which I join in praising him, an aromatic perfume miraculously refreshes and delightfully influences all the senses of my soul."

23. Another time, while <Gertrud>, devoutly kissing the Lord's five wounds, had recited five *Our fathers*, offering them to the Lord in recompense for all that she had neglected to perform of the obligatory prayers and the like for Lady M<echtild> of happy memory, both when she was sick and also after she had died, because her own continual sickness, from which she was then suffering, had prevented it. There appeared five flowers in bloom, as if springing from the Lord's wounds; from them seemed to burst forth, by virtue of the same sweetly flowing wounds of Christ, a balsamic liquid

---

19. *Ex quo omnia, per quem omnia, in quo omnia; ipsi gloria in saecula*, "From whom, through whom, and in whom are all things; to it be glory for ever": antiphon at Lauds for the feast of the Trinity.

of wonderful purity and astonishing virtue. Then she gently greeted the soul of blessed M<echtild>, saying, "O chosen of my Lord, may your goodness accept those flowers blossoming from the overflow of the divine loving-kindness, I beg, in place of all my debts, which as yet I cannot pay. Garland yourself with them for the increase of all your merits, and beseech your spouse for me, unworthy as I am." She replied, "It gives me great delight to look upon those flowers, so honorably associated with my Lord's wounds, for whenever I press them with longing, they forthwith generously exude a most healing liquid from the power of his sweetly flowing wounds, for the absolution of sins and the consolation of the righteous."

CHAPTER FIVE

THE SOULS OF THE SISTERS
M. AND E.

1. Two young girls, more noble in birth but far more in character, related in the flesh but much more closely related in spirit and virtue, after having passed an innocent childhood, were growing in the virtues of the holy religious life. In the fervor, so to speak, of their novitiate they were summoned from this world to the heavenly marriage chamber of their immortal bridegroom. The first had died on the day of the glorious Assumption, the day of her heavenly marriage. The other followed thirty days later, in noteworthy fashion, with such blessed suffering that most magnificent things might be related about the words and deeds of both, for they emanated fervent desire, wonderful devotion, and most excellent intention.

2. Now the first, whose blessed death took place on the day of the Assumption, appeared to <Gertrud>, who was praying for her, as if surrounded by a great light and with various adornments before the glorious throne of Christ Jesus the emperor. But she stood by him like a bashful bride, trying to hide her face and not daring to open her eyes or raise them to the glory of such great majesty. When <Gertrud> saw this, led by loving zeal she said to the Lord, "Ah, most kindly Lord, why do you set your little daughter to one side to stand by you like a stranger, not taking her into your sweet embraces?" At this the Lord, swayed by most gentle serenity, seemed to

stretch out his right hand as if to embrace her. But that soul seemed to draw back from the Lord's embraces as if with delicate deference. Quite astonished at this, she said to the soul, "Why do I see you shrink from the sweet embraces of so amiable a spouse?" She replied, "Because I am not yet completely purified; certain stains make me unworthy; therefore justice decrees that even if I were allowed completely free access, I should draw back of my own free will, since I know I am not yet fit for my glorious Lord." Then <Gertrud> said, "How can this be, since I see you already glorified and standing in the presence of the Lord?" The soul replied, "Although every creature is in God's presence, each soul appears to relate to him in a unique way, depending on how advanced it is in charity. No soul deserves to be fully rewarded with that blessedness experienced by a blessed soul from the enjoyment and sight of the divine nature until, fully purified from every stain, it deserves to *enter into the joy of its Lord.*"*

*see
Matt 25:23

3. Then a month later, when her sister, E. of happy memory, was on her deathbed, and <Gertrud> had been praying for her at length, a little while after her death she saw her soul in a place of light in the form of a young girl who, beautifully dressed in red garments, was about to be presented to her bridegroom. The Lord appeared near her in the same place, in the form of a fine handsome young man, who with each of his five wounds seemed to revive each of the soul's five senses with sweetness of new delight. Then she to whom these things were revealed said to the Lord, "Since you, God of all consolation, are present with her in such gentle serenity, what more could she wish? And yet she betrays an inner heaviness by her sorrowful expression." The Lord replied, "Since I am showing her only the delights of my human nature, she cannot be fully consoled by my presence here, for with it I am repaying her only for

that devout desire for my passion that she experienced in her dying moments. But after this, when she has been purified from the negligences of her former life, she will be perfectly consoled in the presence of my most delightful divine nature."

4. Then she said, "How can it be that all the negligences of her former life have not been sufficiently corrected by the devotion that she manifested on her deathbed, since it is written that a person is judged according to how they are found to be at their life's end?"[1] The Lord replied, "When, her strength failing, this woman was brought to her deathbed, to a certain extent her life reached its end at that time, for then she could not do anything more by her physical strength, but only by her will. The person profits to whom I grant at that time a virtuous will and desire from my freely given loving-kindness. But this does not have such absolute power to wash away all the guilt of past negligences as it would if a person were to correct her life by a virtuous will while still strong and healthy." Then she said, "Surely, my Lord, your most loving mercy would have the power right now to absolve this soul from every obstacle caused by negligence? For you had given her from her childhood a heart that loved everyone and a kind will." The Lord replied, "I shall abundantly reward her heart's loving-kindness and her generous will, but my justice decrees that every stain of negligence must be wiped away."

5. And then, as if gently holding the young girl's chin, he added, "And my bride most willingly submits to my justice, for when she has been purified, she will be most joyfully consoled by the glory of my divine

---

1. *Quia qualem te ultimus invenerit dies, talis judicaris*, "For as the last day finds you, so shall you be judged," Alcuin, *De confessione peccatorum* IV (PL 101:343).

nature." When she smiled and nodded, the Lord seemed
as it were to return to heaven, and she remained alone
in the same place. Raising herself upwards as if with
all her strength, she tried to reach the heavens. By her
being left alone it seemed that she was purified from
having sometimes, through girlish frivolity, behaved too
freely in company. By her trying hard to rise upwards
she was purified from having sometimes, out of physical
weariness, yielded to laziness.

6. Another time, while praying for her at Mass, at
the elevation of the Host <Gertrud> said, "Lord, holy
Father, I offer you this Host for her, on behalf of all
those in heaven, on earth, and in hell." Once again that
soul appeared, raised up a little in the air, with countless
people, as it were, on their knees before her lifting up
something in the shape of the Host with both hands and
holding it out. From this that soul was granted wonderful advancement and incalculable delight. Then the soul
said, "I now indeed experience that what is written is
true: there is no good in someone so small that is not
rewarded, nor is there any sin that is not purified, either
before or after death.[2] For because I gladly received
communion, I now obtain a great advancement from
the sacrament of the altar, offered for me, and because
I had such a kindly will towards everyone, the prayer
poured forth for me now helps me more easily. For both
I anticipate eternal reward in heaven." Then she seemed
to be borne upwards in the air, raised by the prayers of
the church. And she knew that when she reached her
appointed destination, the Lord would come to meet
her with a royal crown in *the multitude of his mercies**
and would lead her to eternal joy.

*see
Ps 50:3; 68:17

2. See also IV.49.5, lines 9–13.

CHAPTER SIX

THE SOUL OF S., WHOSE PLACE
IN THE LORD'S BOSOM WAS
PREDICTED

1. When Dame S<ophie> the elder[1] of blessed memory had received the sacrament of anointing, <Gertrud> was reciting five *Our Father*s for her and last of all was praying to the wound in the side of Christ Jesus that he would purify her in the blessed water flowing from there from every stain, and adorn her with every kind of virtue in his precious blood. <Dame Sophie> appeared in the form of a tender young girl, adorned with a halo; embracing her with his left arm, the Lord kindly carried out in her soul what <Gertrud> had requested for her in prayer. She understood, however, that <Dame Sophie> was still to linger on for a while, until she expiated by her sickness a single fault that she had committed, by offending against obedience in talking with an invalid more than was right. This did indeed happen. For she lived for a further five months, suffering from time to time from such sickness that it was obvious to everyone that she was expiating a fault.

On that very day, however, she manifested a heavenly joy that made it abundantly clear that the Lord had

---

1. An aunt of Sophie of Mansfeld, who succeeded Gertrud of Hackeborn as abbess in 1291.

indeed visited her with his grace. For she strove again and again to explain the gift of God that she had received, but as her strength was failing she could not utter it. And since that one to whom this had been revealed in spirit was present among the others, she called her by name and, stretching out her hands to her, cried out, "Ah, speak for me, for you know!" When she had begun to explain, as if not entirely seriously, the sick woman picked up the story and completed it. And when others added certain things, as if evaluating, the sick woman most steadfastly rejected that but firmly maintained that the Lord had forgiven her sins and had adorned her with virtues.

2. Then after five months, on the day before this sick woman's death, the Lord appeared seated, preparing a restful place in his bosom, in which he paid particular attention to cleanliness and comfort to mitigate the sick woman's discomfort. That sick woman appeared at the Lord's left, as if lying on a bed, enveloped in a small cloud. Then she who saw this said to the Lord, "She is far from fit for such a glorious place as she is still enveloped in this cloud." The Lord replied, "I am leaving her here for a while until she is completely purified and fit for my company." And thus the sick woman remained in her death agony throughout that day and night. But the next day in the morning <Gertrud> saw the Lord bending kindly towards the sick woman with a calm expression and raising her up as if to meet him. Then she said, "My Lord, can it be that you are now coming to the desolate soul as merciful father?" He answered her question with a gentle nod of his head.

3. And after a little while, when she had died, <Gertrud> saw her soul in the form of a girl, as she had seen her before, beautifully dressed in snow-white and rosy pink garments, joyfully flying up to the place prepared for her. When the Lord stretched out his left arm to

welcome her, she leaned her head on it with tender deli-
cacy, as if intending to take her rest. And suddenly, as
if this displeased her, she leaned on the other side, on
his right arm, and immediately raised herself up from
there to press a kiss on the blessed mouth of her lover.
As if unable to reach it, she flung herself on his neck
and placed a sweet kiss on the Lord, between his breast
and his neck. And thus, having slipped back, weary and
panting, onto the Lord's breast, she rested for as long
as this verse was being recited in the Commendation:
The prayer of the church commends <her> to you. At
these words she seemed to draw delightful refreshment
abundantly from that breast, in which *are hid all the
treasures** of blessedness. Sweetly revived by this, she   *see Col 2:3
seemed to draw herself up and breathe freely.

CHAPTER SEVEN

THE HAPPY DEATH
OF M<ECHTILD OF MAGDEBOURG>
OF BLESSED MEMORY

1. When sister M<echtild>[1] of happy memory was
nearing her end and <Gertrud> was praying with the
others, she said to the Lord among other things, "Why,
most loving God, do you not hear us when we pray for
her?" The Lord replied, "Her spirit is so detached from
human concerns that it could not be comforted in any
human fashion by you." But she said to the Lord, "By
what decision?" The Lord replied, "I now possess my
secret in her, just as I once possessed it with her." And
when she inquired in what way she would be released, the
Lord said, "My innermost majesty will attract her." Then
she said, "What death will she die?" The Lord replied,
"I shall absorb her with my divine power, just as the
burning sun dries up a drop of dew." And when she asked
why he allowed her to wander in her exterior senses, the
Lord replied, "So that I may be known to work more in
the inmost being than on the outside." She said, "Your
grace could quite easily persuade the hearts of each and
every one of this." The Lord responded, "And how will
they receive my grace when they rarely or never resort
to their inmost being, where grace is usually infused?"

1. Mechtild of Magdebourg, d. ca. 1282.

2. After this <Gertrud> prayed the Lord that after
the death of blessed M<echtild> he would at least exalt
her with the grace of miracles, to his own glory, as proof
of her divine revelations and an appropriate check on
sceptics. Then, holding the book between two fingers,
the Lord said, "Surely I will not protect my victory without weapons!" And he added, "When it was necessary,
I subjected peoples and kingdoms to me by signs and
prodigies, but in the present case, it is easy to confirm
a carefully considered belief in those who have known
through their own experience of an inflowing similar to
hers. But I certainly do not tolerate the perverse who
attack those writings; I shall prevail against them as with
others." In this she sensed a wonderful sweetness of the
divine favor, with which the Lord welcomes the ready
belief of the faithful that the generous overflow of divine
grace is imparted to the chosen not according to human
merits but according to the unrestraint of the divine heart.

3. And when the same sister M<echtild> of blessed
memory was being anointed, <Gertrud>, led by desire,
saw the Lord Jesus touching her heart with his hand
and saying, "Since that blessed soul, released from the
flesh, is plunged into its source of origin, I shall pour
out abundantly on all those who are here out of love
the swelling waves of my honey-sweet blessedness."
Then, when the aforesaid M<echtild> was dying, and
Gertrud was concentrating on prayer with the others
for a long time, eventually she understood that the Lord
was bestowing a threefold blessing on all those standing
around. The first of these was that he would fulfill the
righteous desires of them all towards him; the second,
that he would tirelessly assist anyone working on the
correction of their failings. She perceived that by the
merits of blessed M<echtild> these two were quite easily bestowed, one after the other, in that place. The third

blessing was that he bestowed a generous benediction with outstretched hand.

4. Then, when she was reflecting upon this with great gratitude, after a while *the Lord of hosts, the King of Glory,** appeared, in form *beautiful above the sons of men,** or rather, above the countenance of angels. He was sitting at the head of the sick woman and was receiving her breath, which, like a rainbow of golden splendor, stretched from the sick woman's mouth to the divine heart on his left-hand side. And when <Gertrud> had lingered some time in delight at this vision, and in the meantime they were reciting the psalm, *O God my God, look upon me,** at the end of that psalm, *To thee, O Lord, have I lifted up my soul,** the Lord leaned over the sick woman with wonderful gentleness as if about to bestow a kiss on his spouse, and after a little while, raising himself, he repeated this a second time.

5. After this, while they were reading the suffrages, during the antiphon *That we may look upon you,*[2] and so on, the Virgin Mother appeared, illustrious offspring of a royal house, suitably arrayed in purple garments. Gently leaning over her son's spouse and holding the sick woman's head with her delicate hands, she enabled the trajectory of her breath to travel more directly towards the divine heart. And while they were reciting, among other things, that short prayer, "Hail Christ Jesu, Word of the Father," the Lord appeared transfigured by wonderful brightness, and the divine countenance glowed fiery red like the sun shining in its splendor. Astonished at this and ravished from herself, when she came to herself after a little while she saw the shining rose of heaven, I mean the virginal mother, press most

*Ps 23:10
*Ps 44:3

*Ps 21:2
*Ps 24:1

---

2. Sixth antiphon for Matins of the Blessed Virgin Mary.

delightful kisses on her son the bridegroom with sweetest embraces, as if in the wild cry of congratulation on such a joyful union with his new bride. From this she perceived that during this time that happy union had been consummated, which had *brought* that thirsty soul *into the* ample *storerooms,** or rather had blessedly plunged it into the abyss of true beatitude, never to emerge.

*see Song 1:3

CHAPTER EIGHT

THE SOUL OF M.,
WHO WAS HELPED BY
THE PRAYERS OF HER FRIENDS

1. When M. B.[1] of blessed memory was in her death
agony, <Gertrud>, summoning all her inner faculties,
was trying to discover through God's grace what was
happening with respect to the dying woman. But for a
long time she could not discover anything except that
she had a minor problem: she had sometimes taken
pleasure in outward things, such as that her bed was
draped with embroidered fabric with designs in gold,
and the like. When she had died, and Mass was being
celebrated for her on that very day, and at the elevation
of the Host <Gertrud> was offering that same Host for
the relief of her soul, although she did not see the dead
woman's soul, she nonetheless perceived that it was
present. So she asked the Lord, "O Lord, where is she?"
He replied, "She is coming to me, dazzlingly white."
She realized from this that all that had been done for her,
in the love of God, before her death had helped her so
much that she had flown up without a problem, because
certain women[2] took on themselves in love her faults

1. The absence of any title such as *domna* or *soror* suggests
that this woman was not a nun.
2. Including Gertrud: see below.

65

that needed correction and through God's grace gave her all their own good deeds.

2. Now when she was about to be buried, <Gertrud> was again praying for her during Mass, and she saw her on the Lord's left, as if sitting at table for a banquet, and everything that was being offered on her behalf in prayer, devotion, and the like was being placed before her in the likeness of various dishes. Indeed, at the elevation of the Host, when the Lord set before her the Host offered for her in the likeness of a drinking vessel, she had scarcely tasted it when she was immediately pierced to the marrow by the innate sweetness of the divine. She was transformed into such a state of loving-kindness that, raising her clasped hands, she prayed for all those who had opposed her in this life in thought, word, or deed, for she now rejoiced in the reward she had obtained from this. And when <Gertrud>, in astonishment, was wondering why she did not also pray for her friends, she replied, "I pray both effectively and lovingly for my friends from my heart to the heart of my beloved."

3. Another day, when she was reflecting that she had completely renounced all the reward that she could earn through God's mercy in the practice of good works for the reward of the dead woman, she said sorrowfully to the Lord, "I hope, Lord, that your loving mercy often looks upon me, naked and poor as I am." To this the Lord replied, "What can I do for one that is naked out of love, except cover him with my own fleece and work with him more urgently, that he may recover the more quickly what has been given away through love?" Then she said, "However much you work with me, I must still come to you naked, for I have renounced both what had been obtained and what would be acquired." The Lord replied, "Although a mother allows her fully clothed daughters to sit at her feet, she puts her arms around

the naked little boy on her lap, wrapping it in her own clothes." He added, "And what then do you have, sitting beside the depths of the ocean, that is any the less than the others who are sitting by the sources of brooks?" That is, those who cling somewhat to their own deeds sit by the sources of brooks, but those who have completely emptied themselves in love and humility possess God, the depths of complete blessedness.

CHAPTER NINE

THE SOULS OF G. AND S.,
ON WHOM THE LORD CONFERRED
SIMILAR BLESSINGS

1. Since, as Scripture witnesses, *by what things* someone *sins, by the same also** they are punished, and conversely in what things someone does good and endures, in the same also they are rewarded, we shall add this account for the profit of our readers. For there were two women sick at the same time; one of them was clearly consumptive and because of this was treated by those who served her with more tender care, as seemed appropriate. Because the nature of the other's sickness was unknown, and so she seemed less needy, she was not given the same loving care. But as human judgments are so often fallible, the one who was expected to recover died more than a month before the other. She had reached her final days sanctified, rather than purified, by much patience and devotion. But the benign loving-kindness of our lover, not allowing even the smallest speck of a stain in the bride so dear to him, purified in her an unwillingness from time to time to make her confession. Although her conscience was not troubled by any sin, she neglected to seek absolution through the priest's words, at least from specks of venial sin, without which human life is impossible: sometimes she pretended to be asleep when the priest was there, so as not to speak to him.

*see Wis 11:17

And so when the time had come that she was about to enter the marriage chamber of her heavenly bridegroom with joy and exultation, her faithful lover first washed away that stain of hers in this way. For she anxiously asked that a confessor should be brought to her, and then she immediately lost the power of speech. Thence she was seized by fear that she would have to be purified after death for her neglect of confession, and thus through that same fear she was purified. Hence the beloved of the heavenly Bridegroom arrived at the celestial marriage chamber with inestimable glory, *all lovely, with not a spot** clinging to her: on this subject the Lord condescended to reveal many things, one of which I shall expound here for the edification of our readers.

*see Song 4:7

When she had been brought before the throne of the King of Glory, he endowed her with this special privilege: he coaxed her with most delightful gentleness to take each of those rewards that he bestowed on her, just as a most sweet mother is accustomed to coax her only child who is sick to take the medicine by which he will recover full health. He did this because she had been afflicted with sorrow from time to time from hearing her fellow invalid being coaxed, although to her they spoke more sternly.

2. After this, the Lord added, speaking to that blessed soul, "Tell me, my daughter, what would you like me to do with the soul of your companion, and what kind of consolation do you wish me to bestow on it? For just as on earth she chose what refreshment she wanted, and you sometimes had to share it with her even though you would have chosen something else, so now it will depend on you what kind of consolation or blessing I bestow on her. She replied, "Ah, sweetest Lord, bless her in every way just as you have blessed me, for I cannot think of any way that would please me

better." The Lord most kindly assented to these words and declared that he would do so.

3. Now a month later, when the other woman had also died, she too appeared on the day following her death wonderfully adorned, as was appropriate, because during her entire life she had possessed a most innocent simplicity, and in addition was very devout and attentive to the strict observance of the Order. Nonetheless it was understood that there was still a stain that had to be purified in her: in her sickness, as was indicated earlier, she used to enjoy certain things that she did not need, that is, gifts and consolation from her friends. And so this stain was shown being purified in this way: she was as it were standing in the doorway facing the throne of the King of Glory, who appeared incomparably *beautiful in form** and most sweet and lovable beyond all human understanding. He caressed the aforesaid soul so much that she was almost fainting with desire to come to him, but there was no way that she could come any closer, as if a nail in that doorway were catching on some of her clothing. And when <Gertrud> saw this and prayed for her out of compassion, the divine mercy released her from this problem.

*see Ps 44:3

4. Then she asked the Lord, "Since that soul has friends among us who are particularly close to you, I am astonished that it seems that it was only my prayers that set this problem aside, although I would be quite sure that they too would have poured out devout prayers for her and would also have expected to be heard by your loving-kindness." The Lord replied, "I have most certainly heard the prayers of my intimate friends for that soul, and have done so more kindly, and blessed that soul more than they could believe, even if they had seen me conveying this soul from purgatory to heaven at their prayers with their own eyes. But I did not make

that problem known to them, because I wanted to dispel it at your prayers. And so they did not pray for her in the way that you did."

Then she said, "How could this be done, as you assured me that you wished to bless that soul in all respects as the one who died before her, even though the latter had served longer in the habit of religion, and in addition had surpassed the other in certain virtues and moreover was brought before you with greater glory without any problem?" The Lord replied, "My justice always remains constant, because *every person shall receive their own reward according to their own labor.*"* Nor can it ever come about that he who has deserved less should receive more than he who has deserved more, unless certain circumstances, such as superior intention, more strenuous struggle, more fervent love, or the like, have enhanced their work. But my generous loving-kindness adds to the reward that is deserved, and also sometimes because of the prayers of the faithful and other meritorious circumstances. Consequently I have blessed them both alike in this way, for I have given both of them more than they deserve."

5. Since attachment to earthly pleasure is indeed a problem that should be avoided, after this she saw that same blessed soul again, not yet completely released from her problem. For she appeared standing before the Lord's throne, and she now desired, with the same desire with which she had earlier desired to reach it when she seemed to be caught in the doorway, to rush into the embrace and be satisfied by the kisses of the one who is *beautiful above the sons of men,** on whom the angels desire to look.** But she was held fast by the same problem, as if unable to bend or turn. When she was again released after a while, she finally appeared, having not received perfect glory, but the Lord seemed

*see 1 Cor 3:8

*Ps 44:3
*1 Pet 1:12

to be holding a crown wonderfully embellished in his hands, and when he placed it on her, she would receive with it perfect glory.

6. She who saw this asked the Lord, "Surely, Lord, it cannot be that a soul is tormented in your kingdom by such anticipation?" The Lord replied, "She is not tormented, but she anticipates the consummation with joy, just as a girl who sees in her mother's hands pieces of jewelery with which she will be adorned the next day at a feast anticipates that day with joy."

7. After this, that soul was gazing upon that person who had poured out prayers for her, and thanked her with great affection. To this <Gertrud> replied, "Although you had always been quite close to me, nonetheless when you were sick you seemed to me to dislike it if I sometimes reproved you." The soul responded, "For that reason your prayer has greatly benefited me, for it was poured out more disinterestedly in love for God's sake."

CHAPTER TEN

S., WHO DIED
WITH A BURNING DESIRE

1. After this, another young girl passed away, who from her childhood throughout her youth until the hour of her departure truly proved by her generous deeds that she had trodden underfoot the world, with all its pomps and vanities, in contempt. When the day of her summons was at hand and she began to suffer her death agony, she farewelled all those present most affectionately and promised that she would pray for them when she reached God, the overflowing abyss of all good things. And when the moment of death was close upon her and she was suffering most grievously, she said to the Lord from the depths of her loving heart,

> Lord, you know my secrets, and you are aware with what great desire I always hoped to expend my strength faithfully in your service, *unto old age and grey hairs.** But now, as I see that it is your will that I should come to you, all that desire has changed to the desire to see you, so much so that for me the bitterness itself of death has changed to sweetness. Hence, therefore, if it pleased you, I would be willing to lie in this suffering until the day of Judgment, even if today were the beginning of the world. But since I know that today is the day that you wish to lead me to eternal rest, I ask you for your loving-kindness's

*Ps 70:18

sake to postpone it, to your praise, as long as my pain may discharge the pains of all the souls in purgatory that you would more especially wish to be freed. And in this, my Lord, you know that I count my own reward as nothing and seek your glory alone.

2. After this and much more, which would be too long to relate, when the infirmarer asked to be allowed to straighten out her legs, which were already as dead, she said, "I shall offer this sacrifice to my crucified Lord." And thus with a violent effort she stretched out her legs towards the crucifix, saying, "I commend to you all the movements of my feet in the burning fire of that love with which you commended your spirit to the Father *with a strong cry.*"* Similarly she commended most devoutly her eyes, hands, ears, mouth, heart, and whole body to God, with the same words. Then she asked them to read her the Lord's passion, and pointed out where they should begin: *Jesus, lifting up his eyes to heaven,** saying that there would not be enough time to finish if they began at *Before the festival day of the pasch.** And this proved quite true. For when she had listened to the passion with the greatest devotion as far as the verse *And bowing his head, he gave up the ghost,** she asked to be given the crucifix and greeted it with words full of sweetest divine wisdom, falling on each of the five wounds; she gave thanks and commended her own soul, which was wonderful and extremely delightful to hear. And then, as if exhausted, she fell back on the pillow and a short time later fell asleep blessedly in the Lord.

3. After this, she was seen to be sweetly embraced by the Lord, from whom she received a distinctive and marvelous adornment, because she had fought so bravely and trodden the world underfoot for Christ so faithfully. Choirs of angels were also heard, conducting

*Heb 5:7

*John 17:1

*John 13:1

*John 19:30

her in a solemn dance, chanting, *Who is this that comes
up from the desert, flowing in delights, leaning upon her
beloved?** When she had arrived before the throne of
glory, Jesus, spouse of virgins, set her before him and
gently said, "You are my glory." Then rising up, he set
a royal crown on her head and thus placed her on the
seat of glory. The next day, when she was about to be
buried, <Gertrud> was praying for her again and saw
her in such great joy and glory that is beyond the belief
of human weakness. And while she was asking her what
reward she had received for each of those things that
she had known to be hers on earth, by her merits <the
soul of S.> won from God that she who was asking this
from her might experience in spirit something of the
blessedness of her reward.

*Song 8:5

4. After this, the dead woman's soul added, "What
more do you want to know about my reward? You need
only know that that heavenly ark, in which *dwells all
the fullness of the godhead corporeally,** that is, the
sweetest heart of my lover Jesus Christ, is unlocked
for me, except for a small section that is not open to
me because I did not earn it during my life. For what
lies there within is unlocked only for those who love
God on earth with such a love that they gladly make
known to the whole world all the good things that they
experience, so that more people may glorify God more
greatly. I did not have this charity, but I took delight in
experiencing alone, with him alone, whatever I received
by his gift. And so I am not admitted to that treasury
beyond delight, which is prepared for such people."
Then she said to the soul, "When my close friends and
yours ask me what I have perceived of your rewards,
what am I to answer, since I cannot express in words
what I perceived?" The soul replied, "If you were refreshed by the wonderful scent of many, many flowers,

*Col 2:9

what could you say in retrospect except that the scent of every single one of them had greatly, or very greatly, pleased you? Similarly, since in spirit you have now received an unaccustomed insight into my reward, all you can say is that my sweetest and most faithful lover has indeed greatly, or very greatly, rewarded me for all my thoughts, words, and deeds far more than I deserved."

CHAPTER ELEVEN

THE SOUL OF BROTHER S., WHO WAS CONSOLED AT HIS DEATH FOR HIS KINDLINESS

1. When brother Seg<uinus>[1] was dying, she had been busy elsewhere and for that reason had neglected to pray for him until his death was announced. She then sadly remembered that he had indeed deserved the community's prayers, as, more than the other lay brothers, to the best of his ability he had always shown himself willing and loyal to the community in his work. So she began to pray the Lord the more strenuously that, for his loving-kindness's sake, *according to the multitude of his mercies** he would repay that loyalty to the community that <brother Seguinus> had shown so often. She received a reply from God's kindliness: "Because of the community's prayers I have already rewarded that loyalty in three ways. For it often did his heart good to benefit someone from his natural benevolence, and now all those feelings of pleasure, each and every one of which warmed his heart after a kindness, are gathered together and make him joyful, for now he experiences all of them in his soul. In addition, he also possesses the happiness of each of the hearts that he ever made happy with some kindness, such as a penny for a beggar, or a

*Ps 105:45

---

1. In German, *Segwin*.

present for a child, or an apple or some other treat for an invalid. In addition I have given him the joy of certainty, for he knows that I welcome these things recorded earlier. Moreover, if there is anything that he needs to be completely saved, it will be promptly provided."

CHAPTER TWELVE

THE SOUL OF BROTHER H., WHO WAS REWARDED FOR HIS LOYALTY

1. Once she was praying for the soul of a certain lay brother who had recently died, and when she asked the Lord where he was, the Lord replied, "Here he is. Because of the prayers that are being devoutly poured out for him at this moment, we have invited him to feast with us, to some extent." Then the Lord appeared as the head of a family, sitting at a table on which there seemed to be laid out all the offerings, prayers, desires, and the like that were being made for that soul. The soul, too, appeared sitting at the end of the table, sorrowful at heart and with downcast expression, as if not yet purified, for then he would deserve to be consoled by joyous contemplation of God's lovable countenance. But he seemed to become a little brighter because he was wonderfully refreshed from the offerings described above by something like steam coming off hot dishes that was wafted towards him.

2. She also realized that in this there was a serious shortcoming: that soul was receiving the effect of the offerings as if indirectly and not in the way that the Lord, after having taken them into himself, serves up with them perfect joy to the perfectly blessed from himself. However, the Lord, drawn by his own kindliness and by the love of the intercessors, constantly made additions of his own, the result of which made that soul supremely joyful. Similarly, the Blessed Virgin too, sitting beside her son in

imperial glory, was seen to place her own contribution on
the table, and that soul received great consolation from
this because he had honored her with special devotion
when still living on earth. Similarly, some of the saints
to whom he had shown some special respect on earth
contributed from their own, according to what that soul
had deserved while alive with greater or lesser labors
or devotions. From all of these, but especially from the
love of those praying, he grew brighter and brighter from
one hour to the next and began more and more to turn
his eyes and raise them towards the most joyful light of
beatifying Godhead, because to have once contemplated
<it> with unwavering gaze is truly to have laid aside the
memory of all sorrows and to have put on the abundant
goods of eternal blessedness that will never fade.

3. When she saw the soul remaining in such a condition, she who was praying for him asked, "For what fault
are you now most burdened?" The soul replied, "My own
will and my own judgment! For when I did good, I used
to take greater pleasure in carrying out my own will than
another's counsel. Hence I now bear so great a burden on
my conscience for this that if the burdens of all human
hearts were gathered into one, it would not seem to me
like what I am experiencing." Then she said, "How could
you be helped?" The soul replied, "If someone thought
about me, burdened for these reasons, and were alert to
similar faults in themselves, it would greatly lighten my
burden." Then she said, "In the meantime, what gives you
the greatest consolation?" The soul replied, "Loyalty, for
on earth I was greatly intent on it. For the prayer that the
faithful are offering for me is relieving my burdens from
one hour to the next; <I am like> someone who is consoled by very good news. And each and every note that is
sung for me during Mass or Vigils is like most delicious
refreshment for me. Moreover, the divine clemency has

added for me from the merits of my intercessors, so that all that they do that is directed to God's praise through virtuous intention, such as working and even eating and sleeping and so on, is also directed to my relief and continual advancement, because I was always lovingly intent on their profit with sincere loyalty."

4. Then she said, "What benefit do you gain because we have asked God that you should be granted whatever good he has performed in us?" The soul replied, "A very great benefit indeed. For where my own merits are lacking, I am adorned from yours." She said, "Since you asked to be promptly assisted by the proper prayers, does it hold you back if someone who is sick puts it off until they are better?" The soul said, "Whatever is postponed through discretion breathes on me with fragrance of such wonderful sweetness that I greatly rejoice that it is deferred, as long as neither laziness nor negligence is involved." Then she said, "When you were sick unto death, and we wanted you to recover and prayed for that rather than that you should be prepared for death as to your soul, did it harm you at all?" The soul replied, "It did not harm me in the least. Rather, it brought the benefit that the more the vast kindliness of God, whose *tender mercies are over all his works*,* beheld you so affected through human weakness by your love for me, the more he was moved by mercy to benefit me." She said, "Do tears shed for you from human affection harm you?" The soul replied, "They do no more harm than <they would to> a friend affected by compassion for his friends whom he saw mourning for him. Indeed, when I have obtained perfect blessedness, I shall delight in <your tears> just as a tender youth delights to see very many people congratulating him with love and friendship. And all this I deserve, because that loyalty for which I earned your love was fully directed towards God."

*Ps 144:9

*Matt 6:12

5. After this, praying for that <soul> once again, when she was reciting the Lord's Prayer and was saying these words, *Forgive us our debts, as we also forgive our debtors,** she observed that soul make an anxious gesture, which greatly astonished her. When she asked what the reason was, she received this response, "When I was in the world, I transgressed greatly in that I did not easily forgive those who opposed me, but treated them sternly for too long. And so to emend this, when I hear these words I am disturbed by the anguish of unbearable shame." And when she asked how long this would continue, he replied, "When my fault has been purified, because of the love with which you all pray for me so devoutly, the divine loving-kindness will be at hand, and thenceforth I shall be the more thankful at those words because God's mercy has forgiven me that fault."

6. Now when the sacrament of the Body of Christ was being offered for the soul at Mass, the soul itself appeared, made wonderfully radiant and joyful. Then she said to the Lord, "Lord, has that soul now triumphed over all that it was obliged to suffer?" The Lord replied, "He has triumphed over more than you or any human can imagine, even if you saw him fly up to heaven from the fires of hell. Nonetheless, he is not yet so completely purified as to be worthy to be consoled by my joyful presence. However, from one hour to the next he is consoled more and more and relieved by all the prayers poured out for him." And the Lord added, "Your prayers cannot help that <soul> as quickly as they would do if he did not have this fault: in the world he showed himself so obstinate and unyielding when it came to submitting his will to the will of those who for some reason were asking him for something that he himself did not want."

CHAPTER THIRTEEN

THE SOUL OF BROTHER JOHN,
WHO WAS RAISED UP
FOR HIS FAITHFUL LABORS

1. Although it is right that souls leaving the body should be purified from stains they acquired that they neglected to amend here, and afterwards should be rewarded for their good deeds, nonetheless God's merciful clemency, as so often, has now revealed its unrestrained loving-kindness. For when brother John, the convent steward, had died, he who had had charge of the community with such daily labors, all his laborious deeds appeared in the likeness of a flight of stairs, on which his soul, having left the body and still to be purified for some negligence, as its suffering seemed to grow less and less rose higher and higher, as if climbing from one step to the next. But since it is difficult to avoid negligence in the midst of many cares, and nevertheless the Lord's justice does not allow even the least fault to remain unpunished, while he was climbing some of the steps on that stair he trembled as if stunned, just as if the step beneath it were giving way and threatening to collapse.

From this she realized that these were those deeds in which he had committed some wrong, and that fault was being purified through the insensibility just mentioned. But when one of the community would pray for that soul in word or thought, immediately a hand, as it were, seemed to be stretched out from above to help, and then that soul was greatly raised up. And after this she perceived that by his loving-kindness the Lord had conferred on that community this special privilege: as soon as those who had in life bestowed any benefit on it by their labors left the body, they earned the right to be consoled, even while their faults were being purified, for the benefits they had bestowed on the community, and the community itself would retain this privilege as long as it did not deteriorate.

CHAPTER FOURTEEN

THE SOUL OF BROTHER TH<OMAS>, WHO GAVE THANKS FOR HIS BLESSINGS

1. The death of our lay brother Th<omas>, who had also been useful to the monastery for very many years with his many faithful labors, was announced when she was confined to bed. Immediately turning to the Lord she prayed devoutly for him and in spirit saw his soul, very dirty and discolored, which seemed to be wretchedly tortured within by unspeakable torment through remorse of conscience. Then, pierced to the marrow by compassion for his wretchedness and reciting five *Our Fathers* in honor of the Lord's five wounds, she kissed them with most tender love for the relief of that soul. And after the five *Our Fathers*, while she was kissing the most holy wound in Christ's side with most devout intention, blood and water immediately seemed to spring from it in an exhalation. And she perceived that the soul for which she was praying, touched by that life-giving exhalation, grew strong and healthy within, but was still tormented by the extreme pain of certain external wounds.

But by the power of the blood and water he was borne to a garden of flourishing plants, which symbolized all the deeds that he had performed in this world. Through her prayers and also those of the whole community, the Lord seemed to have conferred on these plants such virtue that, with a particular plant symbolizing a good deed, by rubbing it on a wound as if with a medicinal herb, he healed it. In this way she perceived that all that soul's wounds would be cured over time, and the more effective the support of the community's prayers, the more swiftly it would be freed from all pains and torment. She also perceived that when a plant symbolizing some deed in which he had acted dishonestly was laid on its wounds, the soul experienced no healing relief from it, but rather its torment increased.

2. Then while they were chanting the antiphon *In the midst of life*[1] in the usual way after his burial, and the community prostrated itself on the ground at those words *Holy God, holy and strong, holy and immortal*, she saw that soul, raising eyes and hands to heaven with profoundest thanksgiving, kneeling at the same time as the convent, and making praises resound to the Lord because he had led him to a place where he had obtained such a salutary result in his soul by his own labors, through the merits of those women for whom he had provided. He confessed that he realized that wherever he had been in the world, he would always have had to earn a livelihood suitable to his condition by his own manual labor; however, he would never have obtained such fruit of salvation in his soul as that which he had now gained through the merits of that community from his own labors.

---

1. *Media vita in morte sumus; quem quaerimus adiutorem nisi te, Domine, qui pro peccatis nostris juste irasceris; sancte Deus, sancte fortis, sancte immortalis, miserere nobis,* "In the midst of life we are in death: of whom may we seek succour but of you, Lord, who for our sins are justly displeased? Holy God, holy and strong, holy and immortal, have mercy upon us": antiphon for the dead, long attributed to Notker of St. Gall.

CHAPTER FIFTEEN

HOW DEVOUT PRAYER HELPED THE SOUL OF BROTHER F.

1. When she was praying for the soul of Brother F., our laybrother, who had recently died, she saw his soul in the form of a most loathsome toad, burning horribly within and tormented by various sufferings for his faults. For it seemed as if he had something concealed under one of his limbs that tortured him unspeakably. In addition, his pain appeared to be greatly increased because he was pinned to the ground as if by a crushing weight, so much so that he could not stand. She perceived from this that he appeared in the form of a most loathsome toad because as a religious he had failed to direct his understanding towards the things of God. And he was burning and tortured inwardly by various sufferings because of the many sins that he had committed. Indeed, she perceived that he had deserved the hidden torment that he suffered under one of his limbs because he had worked too hard to acquire worldly goods without his superior's permission and had also sometimes hidden his gains. But he also suffered the weight that burdened him so much because he had been insubordinate towards his superior.

2. Another time, when she was reciting the psalms and the obligatory vigils, she asked the Lord what relief his soul would obtain from this. The Lord replied, "Although whatever is done to relieve souls in vigils and

other prayers profits them greatly, it nonetheless does them much more good when people pray for them from love and sometimes with few words." It is like this: if someone has muddy hands and pours water over them again and again, they are eventually cleansed, the mud is dissolved and washed away with the water. But if they are washed vigorously, even if using less water, they are cleansed more quickly. So one should know that after many vigils and other prayers have been recited, a single word prayed with love has greater effect and wins much greater relief than if much had been recited for them.

CHAPTER SIXTEEN

A SOUL AIDED BY THE SUFFRAGES
OF THE CHURCH
THROUGH HER PRAYERS

1. A certain person, informed in <Gertrud's> presence of the death of a relative,[1] was so distressed by this that it moved her to compassion so much that she showed herself the more intent on praying for the dead person. The Lord instructed her that Divine Providence had brought about the announcement in her presence to the person mentioned. When she said in response, "Lord, you could have given me the grace to pray for that soul without that sense of compassion," the Lord replied, "I take special pleasure in this work when a person directs their natural feelings towards me with a good will and has thus accomplished a good work."

2. Afterwards, while she was praying for the soul already mentioned, he appeared to her in the form of a toad, black as coal, and contorted from the immensity of its suffering. No torturer was visible, but he was being inwardly tortured in each and every limb by those sins that each limb had committed. Then while she caressed her sweetest lover, importunate in the ploys of love, among other things she said to him, "Ah, my Lord, would you be willing to have mercy on that soul for

---

1. One of the resident canons, according to the Leipzig version.

my sake?" As if caressing her, the Lord replied, "For
love of you I am willing to have mercy not only on that
soul, but also on a thousand thousand souls!" And the
Lord added, "How do you wish me to bestow my mercy
on him? Would you like me to forgive every sin and
free him from every torment?" She replied, "Perhaps
that does not advance your justice." The Lord replied,
"It advances it very well, just as long as you ask me
this with confidence. For as I am God who knows the
future, I have made it fit for this in its agony by certain
<good> intentions." Then she said, "Ah, *health of* my
see Sir 30:15   soul, carry this out as your mercy could prevail,[2] for
thanks to your gift I do indeed have confidence in your
loving-kindness." While she was saying this, the dead
man's soul promptly rose up and stood there in human
form. Having laid aside all his blackness, he displayed
the whiteness of his <still> rough skin with great joy and
thanksgiving, as if released from all his pains.

   3. Nonetheless she understood that that rough skin
still had to be purified to snowy whiteness before the
soul would be worthy to experience the divine presence.
And that purification was taking place in that soul like
this: as if iron blows were purifying it from rust. In
addition, because of the habit of sinning—for he had
persisted in his sins for a long time—his soul found it
as hard to achieve whiteness as the human heart would
find it hard to bear its body remaining stretched out for
a whole year to be bleached in the sun. While she was
astonished at how that soul could be joyful amid such
troubles, she also learned that souls that die burdened by
such great and varied sins cannot be helped by the usual
intercessions of the church until, somewhat purified by

   2. The Leipzig version is superior here: "carry this out according to what it [the soul] could obtain from your mercy."

the mercy of God, they put off that burden of guilt that prevents them from sharing in the intercessions of the church, which continually rain down on those being purified like most saving dew and salve of delight, or draught of sweetest refreshment.

4. Then giving thanks, she asked the Lord, saying, "Make known to me, most loving Lord, with what labors or prayers a person could win from your mercy the release of a dead person's soul from this terrible burden that obstructs intercessions; for I saw this soul, as delighted as if it had been moved from the depths of hell to the throne of glory, in the heights of joy, just because this <burden> had been laid aside. Indeed, I am now to see it benefiting from the church's intercessions that make him unceasingly joyful." The Lord replied: "Only through a feeling of love such as you felt at that time can any labors be performed or prayers recited to afford a soul such great assistance. And just as no one can do this by themselves, except by my gift, so such help cannot be rendered souls after death unless they have deserved it by special grace in this life. Nonetheless, you should know that with the passage of time this unbearable burden is alleviated by friends' prayers or labors, if performed with loyal intention, and <souls> are released the more quickly or the more slowly depending on how persistent are the efforts of the faithful by more loving devotion on their behalf, and also on what they had earned in this life."

5. When the soul so often mentioned felt relief from her prayer, he stretched out his hands to God and prayed that he would accept him in the power of that love because of which he had come down from heaven and undergone death, and, in accordance with that, pay it back to <his benefactors> when they needed it most. Then the Lord, as a sign that he had heard this prayer,

seemed to accept a single penny from the hands of the soul, and put it aside to be paid back as a reward to those who were praying.

CHAPTER SEVENTEEN

THE LIBERATION OF THE SOULS OF RELATIVES OF THE COMMUNITY

1. On the Sunday on which the souls of relatives of the community were collectively commemorated, after having received holy communion she was offering that Host to the Lord for the relief of the souls just mentioned. Immediately she saw a vast crowd rise up from the lowest depths of darkness just as sparks are scattered by fire, some like stars, but some like something else. Asking whether that large crowd was made up of our relatives, she received this answer from the Lord: "I am your closest relative—father, brother, and spouse—therefore my special friends are your very close kin, whom I do not wish to be excluded from the collective commemoration of your relatives, and so they are intermingled with them." And from then onwards she determined always to pray particularly for the Lord's special friends.

2. The next day, during Mass, after the oblation of the Host, she perceived that the Lord was saying, "We have shared a banquet with those *who were ready** to come here. But now let us *send portions** to those who could not yet be present." Again, another year, when the bell was rung for Vigils, she saw a snowy-white lamb, as the Paschal Lamb is usually depicted, and it was pouring rosy streams of blood into a golden chalice

*Matt 25:10
*Neh 8:10

95

as if from its wounded heart and saying, "I myself am about to atone for all those souls for whom a banquet is prepared in this place today."

CHAPTER EIGHTEEN

THE POWER
OF THE GREAT PSALTER

1. When the community was reciting the Great Psalter[1] for souls, which is said to benefit them greatly, and on one occasion, intending to receive communion, <Gertrud> was praying devoutly for souls, she asked the Lord why he welcomed that recitation of the Psalter so greatly, and also why it benefited souls so much. For she thought the multiplication of both psalms and prayers assigned to the psalms for each verse engendered boredom rather stimulating devotion. The Lord responded,

> The extreme love that I have for their redemption prompts me. It is like a certain king who is keeping some of his dearest friends in capitivity, whom he would very willingly set free if justice did not forbid it. Eventually, driven by excessive zeal for their release, the king would doubtless accept it if one of his knights made some payment for their freedom in place of gold and silver, proportionate to their debts, to give him the opportunity to set them free. So I too accept whatever

---

1. A devotion not otherwise known. According to Gertrud's first editor Lanspergius, it consisted of various prayers followed by the recitation of the complete Psalter, each verse of every psalm being followed by a short prayer, and each psalm concluded with a prayer for the dead (Paquelin I.571–74).

I am offered for the souls of those whom I have
released with my precious blood and my death,
that I may have the opportunity of setting them
free from their pains and leading them to the joys
prepared for them from eternity.

2. Then she said, "How welcome do you find the
exertion of those who perform this Psalter for you?"
The Lord replied, "Truly, as often as a soul is released
through their prayers it is as welcome as if it were me
who had been freed from captivity by their payment.
And I shall undoubtedly repay this at a suitable time,
according to the omnipotence of my most generous
loving-kindness." Then she said, "And how many souls
does your mercy condescend to set free by someone's
prayers?" The Lord replied, "It depends on how much
someone's love deserves." And the Lord added, "The
love of my vast goodness prompts me to set free a very
large number of souls at someone's prayer. However, I
assign three souls to be redeemed at each verse of the
Psalter." Then, spurred on by the overflow of the divine
loving-kindness, although she had not yet begun the
part of the Psalter assigned to her because she had been
hindered by sickness, she immediately began it in fervor
of spirit. And when she had completed a single verse,
she asked the Lord how many souls his overflowing
mercy was deigning to release at her prayers. The Lord
replied, "I assign as many multitudes to be set free at
your prayers as the number of times you moved your
tongue to pronounce each verse of this Psalter." Eternal
praise be to you for this, most kindly Jesu!

CHAPTER NINETEEN

A SOUL HELPED
BY THE GREAT PSALTER

1. Another time when she was again praying for souls, she saw the soul of a knight who, I think, had died fourteen years before or more; he was in the form of a huge beast that seemed to have as many enormous horns as other beasts have hairs! And this beast seemed to be poised above the mouth of hell, with just a single branch under its left side supporting it. All the pain and misery of hell, wafting towards it, tormented it with unbearable and inconceivable torture, nor was it receiving the least relief from any of the church's prayers. Astonished at the sight of this beast, divinely inspired, she perceived that this man while still alive had sinned greatly in pride and self-importance, and so his sins had grown all over him like horns and had become so hardened that the soul could not receive the least relief as long as it remained in its bestial hide. But she perceived from the branch on which alone it relied and was supported above the mouth of hell that sometimes, though rarely, he had had some vestige of good will while still alive, through which, with the help of God's mercy, he had been restrained so that hell had not completely engulfed him.

2. Then by God's grace she read the Great Psalter, moved by compassion for him, and offered it to the divine heart for the relief of that soul. Well! straightaway she saw that beast's hide rapidly dissolve, and his soul

emerged in the form of a little boy, still quite filthy. Then when she prayed for him again, he was transported to a dwelling-place where very many souls seemed to be gathered. When he had arrived there, he seemed to exult with such great joy as if he had now flown from the lowest depths of hell to the delights of Paradise. This was because he knew that he could be helped in that place by the prayers of the church, of which he had been totally deprived from the hour of death until the time that he had been freed from the beast's hide, at the prayers of this woman, God's chosen one, and transported to that place. The souls that were waiting there, welcoming that soul with great kindness, seemed as it were to make room for him among themselves. While she was watching this, she was praying the Lord from the depths of her heart's affection that he would condescend to repay those souls for the kindness they had showed that soul. Swayed by her prayers, the Lord soon transported them to a place of refreshment, lovely with various delights.

3. Then she again asked the Lord, "What benefit does our community gain from reciting the Great Psalter?" The Lord replied, "That of which the psalmist says, *Your prayer shall be turned into your bosom.** And in addition, from the abundance of my most benign loving-kindness I shall grant them this additional blessing because of the charity with which they assist my faithful to my praise: after this, wherever in the whole world this Psalter is recited, each one of them will share in it with as much grace as if it were being recited for her relief alone."

*see Ps 34:13

4. Then another time she said to the Lord, "O *Father of mercies,** if someone prompted by your love desired to recite this Psalter to your praise, for the relief of the faithful departed, and could not get as many Masses and

*2 Cor 1:3

acts of almgiving as relate to the Psalter,[1] what could they do to please you that you would accept in substitution?" The Lord replied, "Receive the sacrament of my Body for the relief of souls as many times as the number of Masses required, and in place of the almsgiving, recite an *Our Father* with the collect, 'God, whose property it is <always to have mercy>,' for the conversion of all sinners, and also perform one work of charity for each act of almsgiving."

5. She replied, "May I still ask you this, my Lord, as I wish to be freed from doubt: whether you would graciously allow a somewhat shorter prayer that you would accept as the equivalent of this Psalter for the relief and absolution of the faithful departed?" The Lord replied,

> Say this prayer after each and every verse of the Psalter, "Hail, Jesu Christ, splendor <of the Father>," first asking pardon with this verse, "In union with that supercelestial praise" and so on, and in that love that led me to adopt human nature for the redemption of the human race say the words of the prayer I have mentioned, which relates to my life. After this, kneeling in union with that love by which I, creator of all things, condescended to be judged and to suffer for the redemption of humankind, say those words that relate to my passion. Afterwards, saying these words that hail my resurrection and ascension, praise me, standing in union with that confidence with which, having destroyed the rule of death, I rose as victor and, ascending into heaven, exalted human nature on the right hand of the Father.

1. According to Lanspergius, the petitioner should say, or arrange to have said, 150 Masses or at the very least 30, and should perform 150 acts of almsgiving (see note to chap. 18).

Then asking pardon once again, recite the antiphon "Savior of the world"[2] in union with that thanksgiving with which all the saints give thanks that they are made blessed through my incarnation, passion, and resurrection. In addition, as I said above, receive the sacrament of my Body as often as the number of Masses that relate to that Psalter, and in place of almsgiving, recite an *Our Father* with the collect, "God whose property it is," and add a work of charity for each verse: this I would accept as equivalent to the Great Psalter.

2. *Salvator mundi salva nos*: antiphon for various feasts.

CHAPTER TWENTY

THAT A REWARD, OFFERED UP,
IS INCREASED

1. When she was offering to God every good work that the kindly Lord himself had ever deigned to perform in her and through her for a dead man's soul, she saw this set out before the throne of the divine majesty in the form of very beautiful and varied presents. Both the Lord and all the saints seemed to rejoice wonderfully in this. And the Lord gathered it up very kindly, as if delighted to have something to benefit the needy who had not earned their own blessings by their own actions. Then she saw the most kindly Lord add something from his most generous loving-kindness to each of the works offered him, and thus return them to her that she might receive them doubled, in return for her good will, and keep them as an eternal reward. Through this she perceived that a person loses nothing by helping others in charity but is richly rewarded.

CHAPTER TWENTY-ONE

THE REWARD OF A GOOD WILL

1. One day when they were celebrating Mass for the soul of a poor little woman who was to be buried that day, moved by merciful kindness <Gertrud> was reciting five *Our Father*s in honor of the Lord's five wounds for the relief of that soul. Then, divinely inspired, she also offered the Lord in charity all that the divine loving-kindness had ever deigned to perform in her and by her for the increase of that woman's blessedness. As soon as she had done this, she saw that woman's soul in the place the Lord had prepared for it in heaven, honorably elevated, and after that, she saw her seat raised higher, as much as the choir of seraphim is exalted above the choir of the lowest angels.

2. Then she asked the Lord how that soul had deserved to earn so great blessing in response to her prayers and the offering made for her. The Lord replied, "She deserved it for three reasons: first, because she always possessed a good will and the desire to serve me in the religious life, if she had had the opportunity. Second, because she loved religious and other good people. Third, because she willingly served and benefited them in my honor." And the Lord added, "In the elevation of her soul, you can consider how welcome I find those three things I have just mentioned in anyone."

CHAPTER TWENTY-TWO

THE PUNISHMENT
OF DISOBEDIENT MURMURERS

1. A woman had died who throughout her life had habitually offered many prayers for the relief of souls, but through human weakness had been somewhat negligent in perfect obedience, sometimes preferring rigorous fasting, vigils, and the like to the virtue of obedience. Consequently she appeared as if adorned with various necklaces but encumbered by a heavy weight of stones beneath that adornment, with many many people leading her to the Lord. Seeing this, <Gertrud> was astonished but learned that the people leading her were the souls helped by her prayers, the adornment the prayers' words, but the stones the guilt of disobedience. Then the Lord said, "See how those souls, prompted by gratitude, do not allow me to purify her faults first and show her adornment afterwards, in the usual way, although she must still be purified for her sins of disobedience and self-will." She replied, "Surely, Lord, she acknowledged the reproofs and repented as far as she could at her end. As it is written, 'When man confesses, God forgives.' "[1] The Lord replied, "If that acknowledgment had not occurred, the weight would have overcome her so much

---

1. See Augustine, Enarr in Ps 44:18, *Tu agnosce, ut ille ignoscat*, "Acknowledge <your sin> that <God> may forgive it."

that she would have come to me only with the greatest difficulty." It also seemed that underneath the adornment she had, as it were, a pot cooking furiously, from which the hardness of the stones had to be turned to liquid until it was boiled away to nothing. Indeed, she was being helped by the service of those mentioned earlier and the prayers of the faithful.

2. After this, the Lord showed the souls' path to heaven in the form of a very narrow plank, quite rough, which was extremely difficult to climb. Those climbing it had to help themselves with both hands, cautiously holding the plank on the one side and the other. This signified that one must help souls with good works. Also, those souls that deserve to have angels as sponsors profit greatly. For on either side appeared terrible griffins, that is, demons circling around to hinder the souls. But relief for religious under obedience was to be seen, as if that plank had rails on both sides that could be held to prevent falling. However, where inert superiors neglected to govern those subject to them through obedience, the rails seemed to be lacking and <the souls> were anxiously afraid of falling. But those souls that had shown that they willingly practiced obedience passed over in safety, holding on to the rails with their own hands, with angels helping them and removing all the obstacles in their way.

3. When another woman had died, it seemed as if some sort of hard substance, like gristle, had grown out of her ears, which had to be painfully scraped off with her fingernails until it was eliminated. This was because she had listened to murmurs and detractions. She also seemed to have a gag in her mouth, as if it were covered within by a thick skin so that she could not taste the divine sweetness. And this was because she had sometimes uttered slanders. By this the Lord taught her that

if that woman, who had acted without malice and had quite often repented, deserved such punishments, those who arrogantly do similar things have attached to that skin little darts on the tongue reaching the palate and on the palate reaching the tongue, which create a disgusting discharge by their painful tearing. Consequently they are quite unfitted for the divine presence, since they are abominable to all heavenly beings. Then, groaning, she said to the Lord, "Alas! Lord, when once you used to show me souls' rewards, now you rather show purgation of sins." The Lord replied, "Then people were being attracted, but now they are being terrified, with difficulty, by torments!"

Here we would like to append the consolations on the subject of her own death that God's most benign loving-kindness faithfully granted her.

CHAPTER TWENTY-THREE

HOW HER DESIRE FOR DEATH WAS INCITED

1. On the feast of Saint Martin,[1] during the response *Saint Martin <foresaw> his death*,[2] burning with desire she said to the Lord, "O Lord, when will you do the same for me?"[3] The Lord replied, "I intend to take you away from this life very soon." Inflamed with great desire by these words, she longed *to be dissolved and to be with Christ,** even though she had not previously been concerned with this. Then on the Wednesday after Easter, while still holding in her mouth the Host she had taken, she was divinely greeted in this way: "Come, my chosen one, and I shall establish my throne in you."[4] From these words she became aware that the time had arrived of which, on the feast of Saint Martin the previous year, she had heard it said, "I intend to take you away from this life very soon." Then the Lord added, "However long you live on after today, strive to live not

*Phil 1:23

---

1. November 11.

2. *Beatus Martinus obitum suum longe ante praescivit, dixitque fratribus dissolutionem sui corporis imminere, quia indicavit se iam resolvi*, "Saint Martin foresaw his death long in advance and told his brethren that the dissolution of his body was at hand, for he indicated that he was already resolved": response for Matins of the feast of Saint Martin.

3. That is, inform her as to her death (see previous note).

4. Antiphon for the Common of Virgins.

for yourself, but to augment my praise according to your desire in all things." But since her death was delayed for some time after this, one can speculate that the Lord did not want her to die without the reward for that desire and for that preparation to which he had urged her through those words. For since, as it is written, desires that are deferred increase,[5] it follows that the accumulation of rewards also increases.

2. Another time, one Sunday while she was again reflecting on her desire to be released from the flesh, the Lord said, "If I carried out in your passing all that you could envisage from your earliest years until now, it would be very little in comparison to that grace that I have conferred on you by my generous loving-kindness alone without your desiring it." And the Lord added, "Choose which one you desire: either to leave the body now, or to be made beautiful by somewhat longer sickness, even though I know that you abhor the taint of the negligences <committed> in prolonged sickness." Then, submitting to God's great courtesy, she said, *"Your will*
*Matt 26:42   be done,** my Lord." And the Lord said, "It is right that the choice should be mine! Therefore, if you agree to journey onwards in this poor little body for my love, I shall remain in you like a dove in its nest, and I shall comfort you in my bosom until finally after your death I shall conduct you to the delights of eternal spring." So for a while her desire was moderated. And for some time after this, whenever she retreated into herself, she heard this verse repeated within her over and over again,
*Song 2:14   *My dove in the clefts of the rock.**

3. After this, since she was begging for a speedy release, her desire growing again, the Lord replied, "What

---

5. Gregory the Great, Hom in Ev 25.2 (PL 76:1190A, C).

bride ever hastened with great desire to that place where she knew her bridegroom must cease from increasing her adornment, and in addition where she would not be allowed to prepare any further gifts for her bridegroom?" For after death neither do the souls' rewards increase, nor can they endure anything further for the Lord.

CHAPTER TWENTY-FOUR

PREPARATION FOR HER FINAL JOURNEY

1. One day, about to communicate while suffering from extreme weakness, she asked the Lord if she was about to pay the debt of the flesh as a result of the infirmity that was weighing her down. She then received this answer: "When a young girl has seen the bridegroom's messengers coming more often, and negotiating about what pertains to the completion of the marriage, it is right that she too should prepare herself in those things that make her fit for the nuptials. In the same way it is appropriate that when you experience sickness you should not neglect any of those preparations that you would want to make before death." Then she said, "And how could I know in advance that desirable hour of your coming, when you will lead me out of the prison of this flesh?" The Lord replied, "I shall have two angels from among the princes of the heavenly court cause to resound sweetly in both your ears through golden trumpets, *Behold the bridegroom comes; go forth to meet him.*"*

*Matt 25:6

2. She said, "What then will be my steed when I am conducted along that royal road to be presented to you, my one and only sweetest love?" The Lord replied, "The powerful attraction of divine desire, aimed at you from the depths of my love, will lead you to my realm." Then she added, "What saddle shall I then have, my Lord?"

And the Lord said, "The complete faith with which you await every good thing from my most generous loving-kindness will provide you with a saddle in this journey." She said, "What bridle will direct me?" The Lord replied, "The most fervent love that leads you to long with all your heart for my embraces will act as your bridle." Then she said, "Since I do not know anything else about riding, I do not know what further questions to ask concerning the means by which I am to travel on that desirable road." The Lord, replied, "However much you seek to discover now, in eternity you will rejoice to have found far more, and this is the source of my delight, that human intelligence could never search out anything as great as what I regularly prepare for my chosen."

CHAPTER TWENTY-FIVE

LOVE'S ARROW

1. While a certain friar was preaching in the chapel, among other things he had said, "Love is the golden arrow:[1] if a person has shot something with it, in some way he claims it as his own. Therefore, anyone who neglects heavenly things and lavishes his love on earthly things is a fool." Enflamed by these words, she said to the Lord, "Would that I possessed that arrow, for without delay I would pierce you, my soul's only love, to keep you for ever!" While she was saying this, she saw the Lord holding a golden arrow aimed at her and answering as follows, "You propose to wound me, if you had a golden arrow; therefore, since I do have one, I intend to pierce you in such a way that you will never return to your former state of good health!" The arrow just mentioned seemed bent three times: in the upper part, in the middle, and towards the end. By this she was taught the threefold power that Love produces in the soul by wounding.

2. For when the first section has pierced the soul, it wounds in such a way that it renders almost all transitory

---

1. Ovid, *Metamorphoses* 1, lines 452–567, explains that Cupid has two arrows, one gold and one leaden. He shoots Apollo with the golden arrow that inspires love and Daphne with the lead one that repels it, so that she rejects his advances and is transformed into a tree.

things tasteless to that person, as happens with the sick, so much so that from then onwards that person cannot take pleasure or find comfort in any such thing. The second, in piercing it, makes the soul feverish, like someone who from the intensity of the pain seeks medicine with the greatest impatience; this person burns with excessively impatient desire to cleave to God, since it seems to him completely impossible to live and breathe at all. Then the third, piercing the soul, leads to such inconceivable things that no description can be given other than that the soul, separating from the body, is joyfully plunged into the torrents of the Godhead, delicious as nectar.

3. After the revelation just described, influenced by human emotions, she importunately desired to pay the debt of the flesh in the place just mentioned, that is, in the chapel, as if the physical place would facilitate spiritual things. And since she sometimes included this in her prayers, one day she received this answer from the Lord: "On the passing of your soul I shall cherish you under the protection of my fatherly nature, just as a mother makes her beloved offspring rest in her bosom, covered by her garment, while she sails across raging seas. And after you have paid the debt of death, I shall make you delight in lovely fields of heavenly verdure, just as a mother does not want her little son, whom she wishes to be safe from danger, to be without hope of safety in a port." Then she, giving thanks to God and refraining from that childish wish, entrusted herself completely to Divine Providence.

CHAPTER TWENTY-SIX

KEEPING SAFE THE SOUL'S PREPARATIONS

1. Once in her prayer she was beseeching the Lord's mercy for the hour of her soul's passing. She received this answer from him: "It would not be fitting if I failed to complete with a most excellent ending what I have begun well in you!" And she said, "If you had brought about my passing, Lord, at the time that I thought from your answers I was to die,[1] then I believe that your grace would have found me the more ready, but as a result of the delay I am afraid that I shall be found extremely negligent because of my lukewarm idleness." The Lord replied, "All things have their time in the foresight of my wisdom. Hence, if you did anything at any time, my loving-kindness would keep it safe for you and, whatever you did in addition, it would not be lost to you."

2. In these words of the Lord's she understood that just as it was the practice among the worldly when some nobleman has decided to celebrate a wedding, before then, at harvest time when he is collecting wheat for the coming feast, the rumor spreads everywhere that a wedding is to be celebrated (so, too, when wine is collected at the time of the grape harvest), even though

---

1. See chap. 23.

119

the rumor dies down among the people, these reserves, stored in a barn or wine-cellar, do not dwindle but are served up in abundance at the time of the wedding. It happens in the same way when the chosen are told by inspiration to prepare themselves for death, even though it is afterwards delayed for some time.

CHAPTER TWENTY-SEVEN

HER DEATH ANTICIPATED

1. She had composed some extremely useful guidance on how one should reflect devoutly on one's own death at least once a year and with the greatest possible devotion anticipate its time, as yet unknown, so that she allocated the first day to her final sickness, the second to confession, the third to the sacrament of anointing, the fourth to communion, and the fifth to her death. She decided to practice this again herself, as she had taught it to others, and on the Sunday before those <five> days she called on divine assistance to help her, through holy communion, and devoutly recited the psalm *As <the hart pants>* * with the hymn "Jesu our redemption."[1] In that union in which the loving soul becomes *one spirit†* with God, the Lord said to her, "Lie upon me just as Elisha the prophet *lay upon the boy** whom he brought back to life." To this she replied, "How am I to do this?" The Lord replied, "Place your hands on my hands, that is, commend all the works of your hands to me. Then press your eyes to my eyes and fit each of your limbs to my limbs, that is, in union with my most innocent limbs commend each of the limbs of your body to me, with all their movements, so that they may never move hence-forward except to my praise and glory and because of

*Ps 41:2

†see
1 Cor 6:17

*see
2 Kgs 4:34

---

1. *Jesu nostra redemptio*, hymn for the feast of the Ascension.

my love." When she did this, it seemed as if something like a golden belt came out of the heart of God, which encircled her soul and bound her to the Lord with an indissoluble chain of love.

2. Then around the time of communion, while she was recalling that on the previous day she would gladly have made her confession, if she had had the opportunity, and was desiring to be absolved from all her sins and negligences by the Lord, she saw the Lord putting forth golden hooks or claws from each of his limbs and with the power of his boundless divinity enclosing that blessed soul in himself, just as a jewel is enclosed in gold.[2]

3. The next day, that is, the Monday, to mark her growing sickness she twice read the psalm mentioned before, *As <the hart pants>*, with the hymn "Jesu our redemption," mindful of that union by which the divine nature was joined to the human nature for human salvation. It seemed that the hooks or claws mentioned above as emerging from the Lord's limbs to enclose her soul in him were doubled. On the third day, while she was reciting the same psalm three times in reverence for that union by which Christ was united with the ever-worshipful Trinity for our glorification, the hooks seemed to triple. Then on the Wednesday, while she was commemorating her final sickness with the prayers and the devotion allocated for this, her soul appeared joined to the crucified one, like a jewel enclosed in gold, and it seemed as if from that gold there blossomed flowers like vine leaves that, twining over the jewel, made it wonderfully beautiful. This taught her that the passion of Jesus Christ, in union with which she offered her sickness to the Lord, was rendering her soul pleasing

2. Claw settings were common in later medieval rings.

to the holy Trinity. On the Thursday, while she was pondering her sins in a confessional formula before the Lord in bitterness of heart, all the sins that were being recalled appeared like shining jewels, wonderfully beautifying those golden flowers mentioned earlier from the forgiveness granted by the divine loving-kindness.

4. Then on the Friday, while she was reflecting on the sacrament of anointing, it seemed to her that the Lord was most graciously present and produced a liquid, as if from the depths of his heart, with which he healed and anointed her eyes, ears, and mouth and other limbs, adding as a further adornment the merits of the most holy limbs of his deified human nature. When the Lord had completed this, he said to her, "Entrust this adornment to me, so that like a most trustworthy mother I may keep it for you until a suitable time, when it can no longer be tarnished by sins or negligences." When she devoutly did this, she saw the Lord take that adornment from her soul and place it in his heart, to be kept in a most secure casket.

5. On the Saturday, when she had prepared herself for communion as best she could, during Mass, while the most sacred Host was being elevated, there appeared before the throne of divine majesty four glorious angelic princes. Two of them escorted the Lord Jesus, embracing him with their left and right hands; the other two led her soul into the presence of the Lord. The Lord, gently receiving her, made her lie on his bosom, and covering them both with the life-giving sacrament of the altar, which he held in his hands as if in the form of a veil, he joined them in a blessed union and made them one.

6. And so on the Sunday, while with such devotion as she could she was reflecting on the day of her death with the allocated prayers, the Lord was again present with most gracious gentleness. About to die to the world and to live to him alone from thenceforth to his eternal

praise and manifestation of love, she offered him her limbs; the Lord, granting a blessing with his venerable hand, affixed his seal so powerfully that the sign of a golden cross was imprinted on each one in such a way that it shone brightly from either side of the limb. That the cross was gold symbolized that all the actions and movements of her individual limbs from then onwards would be ennobled by the power of divine union. That it was a cross signified that all stains that she acquired thereafter from human weakness would be promptly effaced by the power of Christ's passion.

7. At the elevation of the Host she was offering the Lord her heart, which was about to die to the world, and was praying that the Lord would condescend to regard her soul, through his own most innocent human nature, as pure and unspotted by any sin, and through his most excellent divine nature would see it as enriched and adorned with every kind of virtue, and through the power of the love that joins the highest divine nature with the unspotted human nature would condescend to render her most fit for all his gifts. With inconceivable love the Lord seemed to unfold his own deified heart with both hands, as if open to her own heart, which was similarly opened to his, and to unite them. And thus breaking out of the most fiery furnace of his deified heart, the flame of divine love, burning furiously, melted that blessed woman's soul completely and made it flow back, having been melted, into God. Then as from the midst of both those hearts, blessedly united, there blossomed a certain tree of wonderful beauty, which seemed to twist wonderfully like a vine as if from one golden stem and another silver one, and to reach upwards with its height, its leaves shining brightly, as if illuminated by the rays of the sun of the shining and ever-tranquil Trinity, which bring unspeakable health and salvation to

all the inhabitants of heaven. And the Lord said to her, "This tree has resulted from the union of my divine will with yours." For the golden stem symbolized the divine nature, and the silver one the soul of that woman with which it was entwined.

8. And when she was praying for those entrusted to her, that tree seemed to bear a harvest of most beautiful apples, bursting with the fire of divine love. These apples bent down towards each of those for whom she was praying, so that through devout desire they might gather them for true salvation. After this, while lying on her bed to rest, greatly weakened, she said, "Lord, whatever I accept from now on as necessities, I offer to your eternal praise, that you may receive them all as if provided for the limbs of your most holy human nature." The Lord replied, "And whatever failings from now onwards you incur from human weakness shall be emended through the power of my divine nature."

9. Then she asked the Lord whether he would condescend to lead her out of this exile through the sickness from which she was suffering at that time. He replied, "Through this sickness I shall escort you to a place closer to me. It is like a bridegroom whose beloved bride is staying in more distant parts. Burning with love for her he summons her, conducting her himself with a vast escort of princes and knights, who all honor her with various gifts and make her joyful with drums and lyres and various musical instruments, and serve her with indescribable pomp and limitless pomp. He leads her with honor to a camp sited near his palace, and when she has arrived, he appears before all his princes and nobles in most serene graciousness, giving an espousal ring as a pledge of matrimonial union. And thus he leaves her there until the wedding day, on which he will conduct her to his imperial kingdom with great glory and honor."

10. "For I, the Lord God, your strong and zealous lover, am with you, and indeed I share with you all the adversities and burdens of your body and soul; in addition, all my saints, rejoicing in your happiness, attend you as you travel along this royal highway. The drums and organs and other sweet-sounding instruments, the presents with which you are honored on this journey, are the various inconveniences and burdens of your sickness, which continually make me sweet music and soothe the ears of my kindliness so that I suffer with you and sway the love of my divine heart to bless you and to draw you closer and closer to me and to union with me. Indeed, when you have reached the place preordained for you from eternity, that is, at such loss of strength that you seem to be near death, then in the presence of all the saints I shall offer you a most delightful kiss and a ring as pledge of marriage: the sacrament of anointing. And through this kiss I shall indeed powerfully infuse you with unction from the profound sweetness of my divine breath; out of its richness you shall be anointed so that in the future no speck of sin or negligence could cling to you that could deflect my most tender glance from you for the twinkling of an eye."

11. "And the more you hasten anointing with holy oil, the more greatly you increase your blessedness. Thus you shall stay so close me that when first I want to prepare myself to conduct you into my eternal kingdom, you will immediately sense this through your understanding because of your closeness to me. Thence your whole being will exult, preparing itself to meet me. And thus, filled with delights, I shall conduct you through the torrent of earthly death amidst close embraces, and I shall draw you far within and plunge[3] you and ab-

---

3. See chap. 7.3.

sorb[4] you in the ocean of my most excellent divinity, by which, having become *one spirit** with me, you shall reign with me throughout all ages. For then in place of the drums and organs of your hardships and burdens, with which you soothed me on your journey, resonant organs will make sweet music for you, as will those varied delights that now caress my deified human nature, in place of the hardships and burdens that I sustained on earth for human salvation."

*1 Cor 6:17

12. After this the Lord added, "If anyone desires to be consoled on their deathbed by a similar visit from me, let them strive every day to be clothed in the most exquisite garments, that is, by imitating the actions of my most perfect life; let them mount the steed of their body, that is, let them strive to subdue body to spirit by following the spirit in all things, and let them entrust the horse's reins, that is, their own will, to my control, with complete faith in my loving-kindness that in all things I shall faithfully assist them in any good deeds by advancing their spirit in fatherly fashion. And let them offer me all their hardships and adversities to my eternal praise. Then I shall make them lovely as if with precious stones and various ornaments for each and every suffering that they endure. But if at some time out of human weakness they happen to take back the reins earlier entrusted to me, let them promptly wipe that away through penitence, and let them once again entrust their own will to me, and the right hand of my mercy will receive them and conduct them with inconceivable glory and honor to the kingdom of eternal brightness."

13. The following Sunday, while she was celebrating that most joyful feast on which, escaped from this exile,

4. See chap. 7.1.

she should for the first time stand before the most blessed
Trinity, and was examining as if in ecstasy all the rewards and joys of each of the orders of angels and saints
with the eye of inner contemplation, and in addition was
wonderfully delighting in the abundant good things with
which they were so blessedly endowed, out of the depths
of her heart's affection she began to give thanks for them.
Similarly she was praising the Lord for all dignity, grace,
and glory bestowed on the most Blessed Virgin Mary,
and was beseeching that Virgin Mother Mary, for love
of her son, that to supplement her own inadequacies she
would condescend to offer to the Lord, on her behalf,
those virtues by which she knew that she was most pleasing to the Lord of virtues.

14. Then the Queen of Heaven, spurred on by the
prayers of her devotee, offered her son her own virginal
chastity as a shining white shirt, her most pleasing humility as a purple tunic, and her own unfading charity
as a green cloak. When the Lord had dressed her soul
with these garments of the virtues, all the saints, delighting in the excellent clothing of those virtues, rose
up and prayed that he would also pour into that soul all
the gifts of grace that any of them could have received,
if they had made themselves fit for them. Then at the
prayers of his chosen the Lord placed on her breast a
most becoming necklace, wonderfully adorned with innumerable jewels; each of these seemed to bring with it
whatever someone had forfeited by failing to fit himself
to receive the gifts of grace. However, this should not be
understood as meaning that one can receive everything
forfeited by the whole world, but that through thanksgiving the soul is fitted to receive, to some extent, what
has been forgone by others.

CHAPTER TWENTY-EIGHT

CONSOLATION BY THE LORD
AND THE SAINTS

1. One time, while concentrating inwardly and pondering the hour of her death, she said to the Lord, "O, how great the honor and consolation of those happy ones who in this life earned the reward of consolation and protection by your saints at their death! I ought not to receive this consolation, unworthy as I am, since I have not rendered worthy service to any of your saints, nor, to tell the truth, am I aware of having desired solace from any saint except for you, sanctifier of all the saints." The Lord replied, "You certainly will not be deprived of that honor and solace from my saints because you rightly preferred me alone to all of them, but rather because of this they themselves feel the more kindly towards you and delight to serve you. Hence, at the time of your passing, when other people usually suffer great anguish, you will have the solace of my saints. Indeed, when that joyful hour has come, at which it is customary to pray for the solace of the saints for others, then I myself, all flourishing and beautiful,[1] filled with all delights, shall appear to you with all the delectability of my divine and human nature."

---

1. *totus floridus et amoenus*: see also III.49.1, line 4, and IV.11.1, lines 15–16.

2. Then she said, "Ah, most faithful God, when will you deign to lead me out of the prison of exile into blessed rest?" The Lord replied, "Was there ever a bride for whom the populace was preparing so great an acclamation who complained of a delay during which her bridegroom caressed her with kisses and embraces?" She said, "What then could you find in me, *the offscouring of all,** in which you could take such pleasure that you would condescend to compare it to the kisses and embraces of a bridegroom's caress?" The Lord replied, "I say this: I give you myself in the sacrifice of the altar so often because after this life that cannot be done. And I take infinitely greater delight in this than the pleasure that all those who have delighted in human kisses and embraces were ever able to experience. For the delight of human kisses and embraces passes away with time, but the sweetness of that union in which I give myself to you through the sacrament of the altar never fails or grows cold. The more often it is renewed, the more vigorously it thrives."

*1 Cor 4:13

CHAPTER TWENTY-NINE

FIRM PROMISES[1] AND PRIVILEGES BESTOWED BY THE LORD

1. Since therefore, as was written above, the Lord himself had prompted her in various ways to desire release from the flesh, and a short while afterwards she had fallen sick with liver disease and had understood from the physicians who examined her that it seemed impossible for her ever to regain her original health, she gave the Lord thanks for this with wonderful exultation of spirit, and slipped in these words: "Although, my Lord, before all delights it is most desirable and joyous for me, freed from the prison of the flesh, to be joined to you, nonetheless if you wished I would choose to remain here until the Day of Judgment and spend my time to your praise in the utmost wretchedness." The Lord replied, "Such a desire has won from my divine goodness as great a result as if you had completely accomplished all that you considered doing."

2. While he was saying this, she saw the Lord overflowing with delights of such unbounded sweetness that a liquid nectar exuded from all the sense organs of his deified human nature, that is, from his eyes, ears, nostrils, mouth, and hands. From it all the saints together drank anew the sweetness of glory, delight, and pleasure. And

---

1. Twelve in all.

*Joel 3:18

the Lord said, "*In that day*, that is, when I have drawn you completely to myself, *the mountains*, that is, the saints, *shall drop down this sweetness*, for then the heavens shall flow with honey throughout the whole world for the increase of your blessedness, and *the hills*, that is, those on earth, *shall flow** with milk and honey,[2] that is, they shall be endowed with the consolation of some spiritual grace because of your merit."

3. Receiving this most kindly answer from the divine courtesy with the greatest gratitude, at the same time, for sweeter increase of gratitude, she began to recall similar promises made her at other times, too, by the Lord, both in person and through intermediaries. For each and every one of them she rendered thanks to God.

4. For among the promises she had received from the most unbounded overflow of the divine loving-kindness was that divine love should indeed consume all her strength. Then, that no death would prevail against her except that most noble power of love that prevailed in the Son of God and separated his precious soul from his tender body. Then, that the decision of the ever-worshipful Trinity had entrusted to the Holy Spirit that, in the same love in which he had brought about in the Virgin's womb the most excellent incarnation of the Son of God in an indescribable way, he would blessedly accomplish by his divine power all that befell her, both throughout her illness and also in her death.

5. Then, that love should serve her, and all those who rendered her some service in charity, either by their love or their actions, would receive as a reward from the divine generosity that God's love would serve them too in their last sickness. Then, that the Lord condescended

2. Antiphon at Lauds and Vespers for the first Sunday in Advent.

to infuse her with as great a grace as any person could receive at that time. Then, that a great multitude of sinners would be converted through true penitence at the hour of her blessed death, thanks to God's freely given loving-kindness. And in addition, that all those who were ever to achieve God's grace would at that moment be made somewhat fit for it. Then, that countless multitudes of souls would also be released from their sufferings at that time to increase her reward and her joy: they would enter the kingdom of heavenly glory with her, like family servants with a bride.

6. Then, she was assured through the ineffable promise of divine truth that as often as anyone prayed for her, they would blessedly experience in themselves the salutary effect that they had requested for her. Then, that as often as someone gave devout thanks or praise to the Lord for the benefits bestowed on her, the Lord would endow the one rendering praise with so many virtues or spiritual graces: if not at once, certainly at an appropriate time. Then, if anyone, devoutly praising the Lord for her and giving thanks, prayed for something through that love, first, by which the Lord chose her from eternity for special grace; second, by which he sweetly attracted her; third, by which he made her one in intimate union; fourth, by which he fully enjoyed her; and fifth, by which he condescended blessedly to perfect her: the Lord would certainly answer that person's prayers, if what was requested were conducive to their salvation.

7. Then, that the Lord swore by the truth of his passion, under the seal of his precious death, that if before, after, or at the time of her death anyone were to comfort her in charity, with good will, or provide her with all those things with which he would wish his own passing to be fortified—and with the intention that he would join

to her all those for whom the Lord wished prayers to be made—and, before the beginning of their prayer, were to offer the Lord his own zeal in union with that love by which he came down from heaven and accomplished the whole task of human redemption, and, after the end of the prayer, were to offer the Lord the same in union with that love by which the Lord suffered death and on the day of his ascension to God the Father presented it with every fruit of his most holy human nature: that person[3] would receive all that anyone in the world had done for her at his own death, as if he alone had accomplished all this for himself with great devotion.

3. *ille.*

CHAPTER THIRTY

SWEET REPOSE

1. Afterwards, Lord Jesus appeared to her on one occasion, *beautiful above the sons of men,** embracing her delightfully with wonderful gentleness and preparing a most delicious resting place on his left arm near his sweetest heart, full of every blessedness. For he seemed to put beneath her, instead of a cushioned seat, all the suffering of his own most holy body that he had endured on the cross for the salvation of the world, so that her soul might draw to herself his most saving fruit, for eternal salvation. He also placed under her head, instead of a pillow, all the suffering of his sweetest heart that he had experienced on the cross, because he knew that his most bitter, most shameful, most innocent passion and death would bear no fruit in so many people. Over these he laid, instead of whitest sheets, that wretched desolation in which he, a most faithful friend, was himself abandoned by all his friends, cruelly seized like a thief or bandit, and mercilessly subdued, dragged to his death, and, in addition, contemptuously mocked, derided, and wounded by his enemies. Then the Lord covered her with every fruit of his most precious death, with which she was sanctified according to every good pleasure of the divine loving-kindness.

2. And while she was resting most sweetly, as if on his left arm, facing God's most loving heart, she looked and saw that deified heart, in which lay hidden every

*Ps 44:3

135

good thing, smiling on her and laid completely open, like a paradisaical garden with every beauty and spiritual delight. In it were flourishing all the breaths drawn by Christ's most holy human nature, in place of greenest grass, and all the thoughts of his most holy heart, in the form of roses, lilies, violets, and various other most beautiful flowers. Each and every one of the Lord Jesus' virtues reigned supreme in lofty beauty in the form of a most fruitful vine, like *the vineyards of Engaddi,** whose grapes are most delightful; truly, these trees of divine virtues and vines of sweetest words, spreading out their branches and leaves around her soul on every side, consoled her with wonderful and indescribable delight. The Lord, too, seemed gently to refresh her soul with all the fruit of the various trees, that is, of his own virtues, and to give her a delightful drink from the sweet grapes. In addition, there issued forth as if through the midst of the divine heart three streams of the utmost purity, which flowed into one another delightfully and intermingled miraculously. And the Lord said to her, "At the hour of your death you shall drink so potently from these streams that your soul will become so perfectly strong and healthy that you will no longer be able to remain in the flesh. But meanwhile, take delight in the sight of these things, to the eternal increase of your reward."

*Song 1:13

3. And while she was devoutly praying to God the Father that he would deign to look upon her through the most innocent humanity of Jesus Christ, pure and unspotted by any sin, and through his most excellent divinity, enriched and adorned with every kind of virtue in which that same glorious divinity flourished through the most holy human nature, she was deemed worthy to obtain the effective result of her prayers. Then while she was praying with the words "Most loving Father, give me the love-blessing of your divine loving-kindness"

and so on, the Lord stretched out his all-powerful hand and made the sign of the holy cross over her. This gracious blessing then seemed to cover her bed in the form of a golden tent, in which there seemed to be hanging drums, organs, cymbals, and various other musical instruments of gold. These all symbolized the priceless fruit of the most saving passion of Jesus Christ, who made her joyful in so many ways.

4. Therefore she took her repose among such great delights, not like a sick woman lying in bed but like a bride delighting in her marriage-chamber, or rather like a soul thirsting for God, who after the kisses of Lia drinks in most eagerly the sweetness of Rachel's, amid embraces so long desired. In this way, while the gentle south wind of the divine mercy was blowing, she was pondering the barrenness of her previous efforts, not in bitterness of soul but as if rejoicing in the good things of her Lord. She went to great lengths to season those efforts with more tasty richness[1] from the abundance of the most health-giving pastures of that lovely place in which she found herself, so much so that she not only paid off her negligences but also added much more seemly beauty to what she had achieved.

5. Then she gathered devout prayers and straightaway composed others even more devout. Repeating them on behalf of all her limbs, she strove first to pay the debts that she judged herself to have incurred for having approached the canonical Hours, the Hours of the Blessed Virgin, the vigils of the dead, and other similar offices without sufficient care. To these she added payment for each and every virtue that she considered she had practised less than was right: love of

---

1. There is a cooking metaphor here. See also V.27.10 above.

God and neighbor, humility, obedience, chastity, sense of community, gratitude, sharing in joy and sorrow, and others similar. Then, to compensate for spiritual exercises in which she thought she had not been sufficiently alert, she added to these praise of God, thanksgiving, reparation, and prayer, not only for herself but also for the whole church. She took great pains to compensate for everything with most devout little prayers.

6. But it was not enough for her to react to each one of these faults with a single act of redress. Rather, as was said earlier, on behalf of the parts of her body she offered for each two hundred and twenty-five[2] little prayers, interspersing *Our Fathers* and *Hail Marys*, because of their authoritative status, and inserting at each one, as was said before, such prayers, sweet as honey, as not only could draw the human heart to devotion but also could attract God himself, king and spouse of eternal delights, to take pleasure in them.

7. But she labored to compensate, one by one, for each of those same firm promises that, as said above, she had received on the testimony of infallible Truth. Although completely convinced by steadfast confidence, nonetheless she never forgot her own unfitness for those things that she believed with complete certainty she would receive from the most generous overflow of God's loving-kindness. With these little prayers, so far as she could, she strove to show herself more worthy.

8. During this she was also rereading her Rule with the greatest care, and weighing each and every word with such devout supplications and heavy sighs that she was able to adorn with most noble beauty not only, as

2. A figure mentioned before, e.g. III.13.2; IV.2.7; IV.23.10; IV.35.10; IV.49.3. We do not know Gertrud's source for her belief that the human body consisted of 225 parts.

said before, what she had neglected but rather what she had achieved with the help of God's loving-kindness.

9. Having completed this with the greatest care through God's grace, she extended all the strength and faculties of her body and soul to higher things. Among others, she ruminated most devoutly on offering God a thousand times over verses that would express the more fervent heat of her desires, and consequently by a more powerful attraction would draw him for whose love she languished into her innermost being and unite her to him. She exercised her intention in this, as loftily as she could, in loving union with the mutual affection and gratitude of the ever-worshipful Trinity, and on behalf of the love of all creation, so that from then on she could ruminate with more genuine confidence on that verse that customarily dwelt in her memory, "Desired a thousand times."[3] <She used to repeat> this verse with others, that is, "Come with haste,"[4] *My soul has thirsted,** "Your conquering love,"[5] and so on. However, she made a pause at the verse, "O most loving Father, <I offer you> that most holy life <in its entirety>":[6] she had received this verse, divinely infused with wonderful potency beyond belief, and she recognized that in a wonderful way the Lord welcomed that same verse from all those who recite it. Thence, as has already been said, she carefully repeated all these prayers throughout that sickness without ceasing because, even though she suffered from a great lack of strength, she did not permit herself to be prevented from carrying this out each and

*Ps 41:3

3. *Dulcis Jesu memoriae*, line 73.
4. Unidentified, but probably from an unrecorded expansion of *Dulcis Jesu memoriae*.
5. See previous note.
6. See II.23.3, lines 8–14.

every day on behalf of all her limbs, unless she were led to higher <forms of prayer> by greater love.

10. Quite often, too, out of the abundant delight with which her spirit was frequently fed, she uttered such sweet-flowing prayers and instructions to her numerous loving visitors that they testified that they had received from this such great consolation of spirit that they served the sick woman most gladly, so that they might be counted worthy to enjoy such helpful consolation, instruction, and preparation that they received through her words. And so some people frequently offered special prayers for her with so great a desire that the Lord would restore her to health, or at least would preserve the sick woman in this life for their own consolation, that the Lord, who never despises the prayer of the humble, because of their prayers undoubtedly prolonged her life in this body, preparing greater rewards for her and rejoicing in their love.

CHAPTER THIRTY-ONE

RECOMPENSE OFFERED
THE VIRGIN MARY

1. She had therefore made recompense with special prayers, as was written above, for having neglected, to her sorrow, various observances owed the most Blessed Virgin. On one particular day she was offering <these prayers> to God the Son, praying that he himself would deign to present them to his most blessed Mother to make up for all her negligences. Rising up, the King of Glory offered his deified heart to his most worthy Mother, saying, "Look, most loving mother, I show you my heart just as it is, overflowing with every blessedness, and in it I bring before you all the divine love with which from eternity I freely predestined, created, and sanctified you above every created being and chose you with special love as my mother; all the kindly sweetness with which I ever caressed you on earth, when you fostered and fed me as an infant in your bosom; and all the faithfulness that I showed with filial love from then onwards throughout all the time that I lived on earth. In all things I, the ruler of heaven, was subject to you as a son to his mother, and more especially in the hour of my death, when I faithfully provided you with a protector and a son in my place, forgetful of my own agony and feeling the deepest compassion for your desolation and sorrow. Above all, <I bring before you> that inconceivably gracious love by which I raised you up above the choirs of angels and saints on the

day of the most joyous assumption, establishing you as
Lady and Queen of heaven and earth. I display all these,
totally renewed and redoubled, for the love alone of this
my beloved, in recompense for any neglect that she has
ever committed in your service, dear mother, so that, with
your blessedness thus redoubled, you may go to meet my
bride at the hour of her death, welcoming her with your
maternal loving-kindness."

2. The gracious Mother accepted this with most
gentle alacrity, and, declaring herself most ready to do
all this, she said, "Now grant me, too, that when I welcome your chosen one according to your good pleasure,
every single thing that you have conferred on me may
cause to flood into her, with divine sweetness, a noble
liquor better than balsam: may she blessedly receive
these things in a flood of ample delights."

3. But that blessed one, disturbed by such great condescension shown by the divine loving-kindness, said to
the Lord, "Alas! most kindly God, that I failed to entrust
to you, with similar devotion, that compensation, however
poor, that I paid for negligences incurred in my canonical
Hours and other duties in your service, since your unbounded loving-kindness has condescended so greatly
to ennoble the paucity of my feeble efforts." The Lord
replied, "Do not be concerned, my dearest, for I have accepted all those offerings in union with that love by which,
eternally ennobled and made sweet in my divine heart, I
inspired them in you. And with them I have joined every
devout intention that a human heart has ever experienced
from my inflowing, and I have offered them, sanctified
most perfectly in this way, to God my Father for all your
negligences, as a most pleasing satisfaction and acceptable
burnt-offering. Thence he too, inestimably pleased, has
bestowed on you all his paternal, or rather divine, love."

CHAPTER THIRTY-TWO

HER DEATH FORESHADOWED

1. At this time it was her custom on Fridays around None to withdraw from all outer things as if intending to rest, so as not to be disturbed by anyone, and to concentrate on God alone with the deepest devotion, by rendering him as if he were dying all that is customarily done for the dying, and also more than could be expected, both in devout prayers and in beneficial meditations. When she had done this for a while with the greatest devotion and had recollected herself again one day as she did on a Friday, she was resting sweetly in great tranquility of mind. The kindly Lord, who is accustomed to add to his great benefits still greater ones, showed her, as if rapt in spirit, the happy death by which he would condescend to call her forth from this world, as follows.

2. It seemed to her that she was dying, reposing in the Lord's bosom, supported on his left arm and resting against his deified heart in the form of a little girl, most delicate and wonderfully adorned. Then a countless multitude of angels and saints flew towards her with unbounded joy. They all held golden censers in their hands, in which they were bringing the prayers and devotions of the whole church to burn to the praise of the Bridegroom, the King of Glory, and the advancement of his bride, that is, her blessed soul. Then while she was invoking the blessed Virgin through the antiphon "Hail,

Mary, that we may be"[1] and so on, the Lord similarly called upon his most blessed Mother to prepare herself to console his chosen one. Then the Queen of virgins, dazzling with new brilliance, bent down and with wonderful gentleness supported the sick woman's head with her exquisite hands. Next, a holy angel was there, this sick woman's guardian, in the form of a most illustrious prince, rejoicing in the blessedness bestowed upon her.

3. Then, while the sick woman was calling upon Saint Michael the Archangel, that splendid prince, appearing with a very great multitude of angels, placed himself at her service and fought off the assaults of the demons that were there in the same place, to beat them back. The demons were in a corner of the building, in the shape of toads and serpents, but so weak that when they tried to raise their heads or make some move against her soul, they were immediately overcome by the glory of such great majesty and fell back confounded, as if senseless, from which she received great consolation. Then it seemed as if there came forth from the mouth of this sick woman the devotion lying hidden in her heart, in the form of *a burning pillar of fire.** It reached up to the glorious throne of the divine majesty with such great potency that that soul now had no need of angelic defense from the harrassment of the attacking demons, since they were so terrified and confounded by the potency of the devotion rising up from her lips that each of them fled, looking for somewhere to hide.

*Wis 18:3

4. And when the sick woman called upon each one of the ranks of saints to come to her aid, as is customarily done for the dying, each choir of saints prepared to serve her with the greatest reverence. For the patriarchs

---

1. *Salve Maria, ut te simus*: unidentified.

came carrying in their hands the fruit of all their good
works, like green branches, and arranged them around
the sick woman's resting-place. Then the holy prophets,
bearing the rewards of divine knowledge in the likeness
of golden mirrors, suspended them on the branches just
mentioned, facing the sick woman; her soul drew indescribable pleasures from this sight. Next came that lovely
chosen disciple, that is, John the evangelist and apostle,
whom Jesus distinguished with so worshipful a privilege
of special love, to whom on the cross he entrusted his
own Mother as sure evidence of his loyalty, and with the
gentleness of a friend he slipped two golden rings onto
her ring finger. All the apostles who were reverently following him, one by one, adorned her remaining fingers
with golden rings that symbolized the special loyalty
with which they had cleaved to God on earth.

5. After this the holy martyrs wonderfully adorned
her with golden bracelets, which gleamed with all that
they had ever suffered on earth for God's love. The holy
confessors, too, offered her delightful golden flowers
that symbolized their most excellent wills, ever ready
to serve God to their utmost ability. In them also blazed
forth with wonderful brightness everything in which
they had ever pleased him. Also the blessed virgins offered her golden roses with thorns like hooks, which
signified the special sweetness with which purity makes
them close to God and binds them with a tighter chain
of intimate vision. For the Lord Jesus, King and Bridegroom of most pure virginity, appeared decked in garments with the same sort of flowers, in number as many
as the virgins who appeared, sharing their own rewards
with her; all the thorns of those flowers were neatly
hooked onto the flowers of the virtues of each, since
<the virgins> attached themselves more intimately to
the Lord God, their lover, because of the privilege of

special innocence. Thence it seemed as if through that closeness each one breathed in a specially sweet experience of the divine. And so when the Lord had bent over her, as if she were attached by so many thorns, since she seemed to be garlanded with the flowers of all the virgins, she too happily breathed in so many inconceivable delights of divine sweetness, and also joyfully experienced what blessedness the goodness and favor (shown because of their bridegroom's favor) of such noble brides could confer.

6. The widows and the other saints offered the fruit of all their good works in the form of golden scent bottles. All the good things in which any of the saints had pleased God smiled on that blessed woman's soul in the likeness of all the presents that each was offering, and shone on her soul as if she alone had performed them all. From this she was inconceivably consoled.

7. The Holy Innocents, although they seemed to possess little of their own, nonetheless out of reverence for their Lord rejoiced that they had been redeemed by his precious blood and had received the eternal kingdom through his generous loving-kindness. They did not fail to honor her with their favor, but shone upon her soul with brightest splendor of their purest innocence, ennobled in union with the supremely worthy innocence of Christ Jesus, and made it wonderfully beautiful.

8. Then the Son of the highest God, the King of Glory, bending down with incalculable gentleness, was about to offer a kiss to his bride, luxuriating in his bosom. He drew in that most blessed soul completely by his divine virtue, just as the brilliant noonday heat attracts and evaporates a tiny drop of dew,[2] with the

---

2. See V.7.1.

fruit of all the virtues and good deeds that had been offered her by all the saints in the form of the presents just described. And thus, completely engulfing and permeating her, he made her like himself, just as fire transforms iron.

CHAPTER THIRTY-THREE

THE COMMENDATION
OF THIS BOOK

1. When this book had been written down, the Lord appeared to her, holding it clasped to his breast, and said, "I have clasped this book of mine to the inmost recesses of my divine breast, to permeate all the letters written in it through and through with the sweetness of my divinity, just as sweetest mead strongly permeates a piece of fresh white bread, so that everyone who reads it to my praise with humble devotion will obtain from it the fruit of eternal salvation." Then she prayed the Lord that he would deign to preserve the book from every error, to his praise and glory. Stretching out his venerable hand above it, he protected it with the sign of the holy cross, saying, "With that same power by which in this Mass I transformed bread and wine for the salvation of all, I have also just sanctified with my heavenly blessing all that is written down in this book for all those, as I said before, desiring to read it with humble devotion for true salvation."

And the Lord added, "The scribe's labor pleases me in this way, as if she had hung up as many scent bottles[1] to adorn me as the letters that she wrote! I am wonderfully delighted by each and every one of them

---

1. See also IV.12.2 and V.32.6.

in three ways. For truly I taste in them the ineffable sweetness of my divine love, from which flows all that is written in it. Also, the sweet scent of the writer's good will sways me. And the depiction of my generous loving-kindness, which is evident in all that is written in the book, delights me. For in the same love with which I inspired in you all that is written in this book by my generous loving-kindness, entrusting those same things, also in the same love, to the memory of the one who listened to you,[2] I composed, arranged, and wrote it all according to my best pleasure, using her hands. So with my most holy life I shall make a covering for that book that I have repeatedly called mine, and I shall furnish it with the rosy jewels of my five wounds, and with the

*Rev 6:1   seven gifts of the Holy Spirit, like *seven seals,* * I shall seal it with my divine power, so that *no one can deliver*

*see Job 10:7   *it out of my hand.*" *

---

2. That is, Sister N.

CHAPTER THIRTY-FOUR

THE ACCEPTABILITY
OF THIS BOOK

1. After this on another occasion when the compiler was about to receive communion, she was carrying this book under her cloak hidden in her sleeve, to offer it to the Lord to his eternal praise without anyone's knowledge. When she knelt in her usual way and bowed deeply before the Lord's Body, someone else saw the Lord gently embrace her with great joy, as if from the unrestraint of overflowing love, as she knelt before him. He said, "I shall penetrate all the words of this book just offered me with the sweetness of my divine love and by penetrating will make it fertile, for it has indeed been composed faithfully at the prompting of my spirit. And if anyone comes to me with humble heart and wishes to read it for love of my love, truly I shall point out to that person <sitting> on my lap, as if with my own finger,[1] whatever is useful for them one by one. In addition, I shall bend down to them so graciously that just as someone full fed with various spices breathes upon the one who wishes to kiss him with his breath, so I will powerfully instill that soul's sure salvation with the breath of my divine nature. But if anyone, prompted by vain curiosity, comes up behind me, looks at the book as if

---

1. See IV.5.3, lines 21–24.

leaning on my shoulder, and turns its text upside down while perusing it, I shall not hesitate to confound them by my divine power and cast them off, since I would certainly not wish to support their weight for long!"

CHAPTER THIRTY-FIVE

THE OFFERING OF THIS BOOK

1. I offer you, Christ Jesu, primal light of eternal lights,[1] this nectar-sweet torrent of your generous loving-kindness that the powerful sweetness of your unsearchable divine nature has brought forth from the depths of your loving heart to inundate, water, fertilize, and bless the heart and soul of your chosen, to draw her and bind her indissolubly to yourself. I do this in union with that most excellent charity by which you, the Only-Begotten of the highest Father, diverted back to the abyss of its origin with abundant thanksgiving all that had flowed from your divine nature into your deified human nature. I pray with the loving desire of every creature that you should draw <this book> to yourself, through the power of your sweet-flowing spirit, for your eternal, immeasurable, and unchanging praise, just as your unfathomable wisdom on high knows that it befits the superexcellent omnipotence of God the Father and pleases the sweet benevolence of the Holy Spirit. <I offer this> as full and sufficient thanksgiving for all blessedness that you have worked through the same Spirit, are working, and deign to work for ever in the heart and soul of anyone who receives <it>; and also of all those who until the end of the world will take from

---

1. See PsAnselm (Eckbert of Schönau), *Meditation* 13 (PL 158:778).

it any enlightenment, comfort, or instruction, according to your faithful promise, or at least would receive them if your goodness, my God, had found them capable; and as worthy satisfaction for all those things in which the poverty of my understanding, my inadequate zeal, and my ineptitude failed sufficiently to elucidate and explain your gifts that had been entrusted to me to distribute, and for all those who out of human weakness, or diabolical instigation, will disregard and trample under foot your freely flowing loving-kindness that in it shines brightly, smells delightfully, and tastes sweetly—which I hope will not happen, thanks to your mercy. And I offer it to obtain effectively all grace that could be obtained through the love and favor of the divine heart by all those who with humble devotion for love of your love deign to read it through with loving gratitude, and are sedulous to imitate whatever is useful in it for reverence of you from whom it has proceeded.

2. And also because your unfathomable goodness, God of my heart, has deigned to choose me, smallest particle of extreme worthlessness, or rather, to speak more truly, outcast of all your creation, to oversee its most noble distribution, although my insignificance could in no way be equal to the task, I offer you your sweetest, and uniquely worthy, heart, as complete in that worthiness, excelling in divine favor and perfection of every kind of blessedness.

CHAPTER THIRTY-SIX

CONCLUSION

1. This book was composed to the praise and glory of God, lover of human salvation, but very many, or, rather, countless things having been omitted for the sake of brevity, it has been completed with such obvious and, so to speak, miraculous help from the divine mercy, because in no other way could it make known what abundant harvest of souls he himself, who goes before and follows after the best of gifts, expects of it. However, the stream of divine inflowings directed at his chosen one has by no means been exhausted, but what is appropriate for us has been shared with us. Leading his chosen one as if by the upward steps of images, he conducted her to more hidden things, or rather to purer and more excellent draughts of wisdom, which the shadows of corporeal images could by no means bring to common knowledge. May God's most unbounded loving-kindness, however, render all these, together with everything that is written here for the salvation of those in need, so abundantly fertile that, the harvest having been increased a hundredfold, <the needy> may be found worthy to be written in the book of life. And meanwhile, may the less experienced readers of this book, who are not strong enough to swim in the fast-flowing waters of the divine loving-kindness by their own efforts, at least secure their passage on this ship. Delighting in the gentle guidance, as it were, of

*see Ps 33:9

*Ps 54:23

the blessings bestowed on their fellow, by making time for reading, meditation, and contemplation, they may themselves finally begin to taste *how sweet is the Lord,** and how truly blessed is the one who hopes in him and *casts* all his thoughts *upon him.** By his goodness may he who lives and reigns in the perfect Trinity for ever and ever deign to grant us this! Amen.

Glory, majesty, strength, honor, and power
Be now to you, O Christ, for this book has come to
an end.
Pray for the scribe.

THE MASS PERSONALLY SUNG IN HEAVEN BY THE LORD JESUS FOR A CERTAIN VIRGIN CALLED TRUTTA WHILE SHE WAS STILL ALIVE

1. On the Sunday *Gaudete in Domino,*[1]* when this virgin was wishing to communicate, and during the first Mass, which was "Drop down dew,"[2]* inwardly sorrowing she complained to the Lord that she could not hear Mass. The almighty Lord, taking pity on his wretch, gently comforted her, saying, "Do you want me to sing Mass for you myself, beloved?" She replied, "Yes indeed, O my soul's sweetness, I pray for this whole-heartedly as a suppliant." "And what Mass would you like to hear?" said the Lord. "Whatever you decide to sing." "Surely," said the Lord, "you do not want to hear 'In the midst of the church'?"[3] "No," she replied. And when the Lord had suggested some more Masses to her by name and she had rejected all of them, the Lord finally asked her whether she would like to hear "The Lord has said to me."[4]* She refused it in the same way.

*Phil 4:4

*Isa 45:8

*Ps 2:7

1. Third Sunday in Advent, so called from the opening words of the Office, "Rejoice in the Lord." See also II.5.1.
2. Votive Mass of the Virgin in Advent.
3. Introit for the feast of Saint John the Evangelist, or Common of an Evangelist.
4. Introit for Christmas (Midnight Mass).

The Lord said to her, "At each and every word of that introit I could certainly endow you with such understanding that you would be marvelously comforted from it." But while she inwardly considered how this could be, as the words of that introit seemed to apply to the Only-Begotten of God the Father alone, the Lord together with all the saints intoned with a loud voice the introit of the current Sunday, saying, "Rejoice in the Lord always," provoking her joyfully to delight in him. And the Lord was seated on the throne of his royal majesty, and, falling down, her soul sweetly kissed his feet.

2. Then with a clear voice he added, "Lord have mercy, God of great power, liberator of humanity."[5] Well! two shining princes from the choir of thrones came forward, gathering up that soul and leading her into the presence of God the Father; falling on her face at once, prostrate she adored him. During the first "Lord have mercy" God the Father kindly granted full remission of all the sins that she had committed from human weakness. After this the princes already mentioned raised her soul to its knees. In this way during the second "Lord have mercy" she was privileged to receive forgiveness for all the sins that she had committed out of human ignorance. Then the princes again lifted her up and, standing, she bowed down as if to kiss the Lord's feet and received remission for all the sins that she had committed out of ill-will. Next, two glorious leaders from the order of cherubim came forward and, encircling her soul, conducted it to the Son of God. Gently receiving her amid sweet embraces, he pressed her to his divine heart.

3. Then her soul, through desire, drew to herself all the pleasure that anyone had ever felt in human em-

5. Trope (amplification) of the Kyrie.

braces, and during the first "Christ have mercy" she poured this back from her heart into the divine heart, as if into the very source from which proceeded every delight of the whole of creation. This happened through a wonderful in-flowing of God into her soul and a re-ciprocal flowing back of her soul into God, so that at each descending note the divine heart flowed into her soul with indescribable pleasure, and at each ascending note her soul flowed back into God with every delight. At the second "Christ have mercy," her soul drew into herself every delight in kissing that anyone had ever experienced, and similarly offered it to her best beloved through a sweet kiss that she pressed on his mouth, flow-ing with honey. Then at the third "Christ have mercy" the Son of God, stretching out his hands, joined all the fruit of his own most holy life to the works of that soul.

4. Finally, two exalted princes from the choir of seraphim came forward, bearing up that soul, and rev-erently presented her to the Holy Spirit. Passing through the three faculties of her soul, during the first "Lord have mercy" he illuminated the rational faculty of her soul with the splendor of his divinity, to know his most praiseworthy will in all things. During the second, he strengthened the irascible faculty to resist all the strat-agems of the enemy and overcome all evil. And during the last "Lord have mercy," he inflamed the concupi-scible faculty of her soul so that she might love God passionately *with her whole heart and with her whole soul and all her strength.** That the seraphic spirits, who are highest among the angelic orders, led her soul to the presence of the Holy Spirit, who is the Third Person in the Holy Trinity; that the thrones presented her to God the Father; and that the cherubim presented her to the Son, who lives and reigns in the perfect Trinity for ever and ever, indicated that "the Godhead of the Father and

*see
Luke 10:27

of the Son and of the Holy Spirit is all one, the glory equal, the majesty co-eternal."[6]

5. Then the Son of God rose up from his royal throne and turned towards God the Father; singing most sweetly, he intoned "Glory to God in the highest," in that word "Glory" praising the vast and incomprehensible power of God the Father. Drawing that phrase "in the highest" to himself, he lauded his own unsearchable and unutterable wisdom. In those words "to God," he honored the incalculable and ineffable sweetness of the Holy Spirit. Then all the court of heaven joined in and sang with sweet-sounding voices, "And on earth, peace to his people of good will." Then the Son of God resumed his seat once more. Throwing herself at his feet, her soul remained there, recognizing and despising her own worthlessness. The Lord most courteously bent down and drew her to him with his worshipful hand. Immediately rising up and standing before the Lord, she was completely illuminated in a miraculous way with the brightness of divine splendor. Well! two brilliant princes from the order of thrones arrived bearing a wonderfully decorated throne, and putting it down before the Lord, they held it reverently. Then two illustrious leaders from the choir of seraphim caught up the soul and placed her on that throne, lovingly supporting her from right and left. Also, two glorious princes from the order of cherubim, carrying two torches, stood before the soul. And thus, seated in glory before her beloved, she seemed to shimmer in royal purple with a beauty like his. But whenever the celestial hosts reached any words in their chanting that applied to God the Father, such as "Lord God, heavenly King," they immediately fell silent in

6. Athanasian Creed verse 6.

unison, and then the Son of God alone chanted them
to God's praise and glory with the greatest reverence.

6. When "Glory <to God> in the highest" was finished, the Lord Jesus, High Priest and true pontiff, rose
up and sweetly greeted the soul, chanting, "The Lord be
with you, beloved." The soul joyfully responded with
"And may my spirit be with you, best beloved." At this,
bending down to the ground with the greatest thankfulness, the Lord gave the soul thanks because she had
prepared herself to join her spirit to the divine nature
of the one whose *delights are to be with the children of
men and women.** Then, continuing, the Lord recited   *see Prov 8:31
the Collect, "God, who has enlightened this most sacred
night with the brightness of the true light."[7] He ended
this by saying, "through Jesus Christ your Son," as if
giving thanks to God the Father for that soul's enlightenment, whose worthlessness was indicated by the word
night, but who was also called "most sacred" because
she was miraculously ennobled by recognition of her
own worthlessness.

7. Then that vigorous and lovely youth John the
Evangelist, who is glorified for *leaning on the Lord's
breast,** rose up, dressed in yellow garments, woven all   *John 13:25
over with golden eagles.[8] Standing between the bridegroom and bride, that is, between God and that soul,
and turning one side towards the Lord and the other
towards the soul, he clearly chanted the epistle, saying,
"This is the bride." Then the entire company of all the
saints chanted in conclusion, *To him be glory for ever.**   *Rom 11:36
After this they all sang the gradual, "With your comeli-
ness and your beauty,"[9]* adding the verse, *Hearken, O*   *Ps 44:5

7. Collect for Midnight Mass on Christmas Day.
8. Cf. IV.4.1.
9. Common of Virgins.

*Ps 44:11

*2 Cor 11:2

*see
Luke 10:21
†see
1 John 4:8

*Luke 10: 21

*daughter, and see.** And when after this they had added "Alleluia," Paul, outstanding doctor, pointing at that soul with his right index finger, added, *I am jealous of you.*[10]* And so the entire heavenly host continued the rest in unison, adding the sequence *Let the daughters of Sion rejoice*[11] in honor of that soul. In all this she understood and perceived wonderful and indescribable delights.

8. While they were chanting this verse in the sequence, "When she did not consent" and so on, the soul, judging that she had been too negligent in resisting a certain temptation, tried to hide her face as if from shame. But the Lord, that soul's most chaste and zealous supporter, not able to bear his bride's shame, promptly and completely concealed that negligence with a golden necklace, wrought most miraculously, which symbolized his own most glorious victory with which he had powerfully overcome all the assaults of the enemy. Then another evangelist came forward and began the gospel, *The Lord Jesus rejoiced in the Holy Spirit and said.** At these words *God, who is charity,*† spurred on by the goads of unrestrained love and piercingly excited[12] by the sweetness of his divine nature, rose up and, raising his hands, chanted the rest of the gospel with sweetest melody, saying, *I confess to you, Father, lord of heaven and earth <because you have hidden these things from the wise>,** reminding the heavenly Father with what great fervor of heart and thankfulness he spoke those words on earth. And during each and every one of those words he gave special thanks for all the blessings that

10. The full verse makes the relevance of this text clear: "For I am jealous of you with the jealousy of God. For I have espoused you to one husband that I may present you as a chaste virgin to Christ."
11. Sequence for feasts of Virgins.
12. *pertransitive commotus*: see also III.44.1, lines 10–11.

had been or would be lavished on that soul who was privileged to be there.

9. When the gospel was finished, the Lord indicated to the soul that in the person of the church, making public declaration of the catholic faith, she should chant, "I believe in one God." When she had done this, the choir of saints followed and chanted the offertory, "Lord God, *in the simplicity of my heart,*"[13]* adding, "*Moses sanctified <an altar to the Lord>.*"[14]* While they were singing this, the uniquely worthy heart of the Lord Jesus seemed to project from his chest like a golden altar wonderfully sparkling with fiery splendor. Then all the angels who were assigned to the service of men and women took flight and with great joy offered living birds on that altar of the Lord's heart, which signified all the good deeds and prayers and the like performed by those entrusted to them. Then all the saints came forward and one by one joyfully offered their own merits to their Lord on that same altar, for eternal praise and for the salvation of that soul there present. Last of all came a magnificent prince, that is, the angel assigned to her protection by the Lord; he was carrying a golden chalice that he similarly offered on the golden altar of the divine heart as a sacrifice. In it were all the trials, troubles, and burdens, both physical and mental, that that blessed one had endured from her childhood. At once, like a priest consecrating the Host, the Lord blessed this chalice with the sign of the cross. When this had been done, he intoned the words, "Lift up your hearts" with sweet

*1 Chr 29:17
*see
Exod 19:14

---

13. *Domine Deus, in simplicitate cordis mei laetus obtuli universa, et populum tuum qui repertus est vidi cum ingenti gaudio: Deus Israel, custodi hanc voluntatem,* Offertory for the feast of the Dedication of the Church.

14. Offertory for the 18th Sunday after Pentecost.

voice. At that, all the saints, having been summoned, came forward and, lifting up their hearts in the likeness of golden pipes, placed them by the golden altar of the divine heart, so that they might be privileged to receive some little drops from the overflow of that chalice that the Lord had blessed and consecrated with such care, to the increase of their reward, their joy and their glory.

10. Then the Son of God continued, sweetly chanting "Let us give thanks" and "It is indeed right" to the praise and glory of God the Father, with most intent devotion and in thanksgiving for all the blessings that had been or would be lavished on this chosen one, now and in the future. And when he had chanted "through Jesus Christ" in the preface, he fell silent for a while, and the whole host of heaven with most loud and reverent jubilation made the words "our Lord" resound, as if they were declaring with unspeakable joy that he alone was the Lord God, creator and redeemer and most generous giver of all good things, to whom alone is owed all honor and glory, praise and jubilation, power and authority, and the allegiance of all creation. And while they were chanting, "Whom the angels praise,"[15] all the angelic spirits flew to and fro in an indescribable dance, clapping their hands as if encouraging the celestial court to praise the Lord. At that phrase "the dominions worship," the same choir fell on its knees and worshiped the Lord, confessing that to him alone *every knee should rightly bow, of those that are in heaven, on earth, and under the earth.* Adding "the powers tremble," the entire order of powers quickly fell on its face, to testify that he alone should be revered by every creature. And

*2 Phil 2:10

15. These words, and the four subsequent quotations, are from *Eterne Deus, qui salutem humani generis*, the proper preface for various feasts.

saying, "the heavens, and the heavenly virtues, and the blessed seraphim," they joined together with the other orders of angels in singing with an inconceivably sweet sound and praising the Lord. Then the whole host of saints, rejoicing together in sweet harmony, made re-echo the words, "with whom, we pray, may you command that our voices too may be joined."

11. Then the radiant rose of heavenly beauty, the Virgin Mary, blessed above all creatures, came forward and sweetly intoned, "Holy, holy, holy," in these three words praising with greatest thankfulness the incomprehensible omnipotence and unsearchable wisdom and sweetest benevolence of the supreme and undivided Trinity. At the same time she stirred the entire heavenly host to wish her joy because she was the most express *image of God,** most powerful after God the Father, **see Col 1:15* most wise after the Son, and made most kindly after the Holy Spirit the Paraclete.[16] Then all the saints continued, saying, "Lord God of Sabaoth" and so on. When this was finished, the Lord Jesus, true priest and supreme pontiff, rising up from his imperial throne, with his own hands seemed to lift up his most holy heart, which <Gertrud> compared to a golden altar,[17] presented it to God the Father, and seemed to sacrifice himself on it in such an indescribable and incomprehensible way that no created being, however worthy, could hope to understand it at all.

12. In that very same time that the Son of God offered his divine heart to God the Father, the bell was ringing in the church at the elevation of the Host. So it came about that at one and the same moment the Lord was accomplishing in heaven what the service of the

16. See also IV.12.4, lines 7–9.
17. See *Mass*, 9, above.

priest was doing on earth, although she was completely oblivious of the time or of what was being chanted in the Mass. And while her soul was delighting greatly in wonder at such incomprehensible divine working, he indicated to her that she should recite "Our Father" in that union in which that prayer had been imbued with sweetness for so long in his sweetest heart and offered out of such great love for the salvation of all the faithful. When she had recited it to the end, receiving this from her most gladly, the Lord gave it to all the angels so that they might achieve with that "Our Father" all that they could ever achieve through any prayer, for the salvation of the whole church and also of the faithful departed.

13. Then the Lord again indicated to her soul that she should pray for the church. And when she was praying most devoutly for all in general and for individuals in particular, the Lord shared that prayer with the universal church, in union with all the prayers and deeds of his most holy human nature, with as great a result as one could ever obtain from any prayer. He said, "That prayer that you just offered me for the church will be, in a way beyond understanding, its abundant "salvation of salvations" (just as one says, "song of songs") because of its sublimity." Then she said, "Ah, my Lord, when will the <wedding> banquet take place?" The Lord gently replied, "Not only will you perceive this with the ears of your heart, but you will also sweetly sense it in all the innermost recesses of your soul." And calling her to him, and pressing her in his bosom with lovely embraces, and smothering her with sweetest kisses, he flowed into her with such great condescension, wonderfully penetrating her with the power of his divine nature. Drawing her again to himself in return, transporting her into himself, and making himself one with her, he made her blessed, as far as is possible on earth to enjoy this

happy experience. And thus he united her to himself sacramentally in such a union by the reception of his most holy Body and Blood.

14. And when she had communicated, the "cantor of cantors," or rather the most ardent supporter of his loved ones, piercingly intoned, "Behold: what I have desired, now I see; what I have hoped for, now I hold; I am united in spirit with the one whom I loved with complete devotion when I was on earth."[18] In that phrase "when I was on earth," he openly declared that he would have endured all the labors, trials, and tribulations that he had borne on earth for the salvation of this soul alone. If he could have obtained no other result from his most holy life in its entirety, his most innocent passion and most bitter death, he would deem himself sufficiently satisfied in the pleasure, so much desired, of that union that he had at that moment accomplished in that soul. O inestimable sweetness of the divine condescension, so eager to take pleasure in a human soul, that he who would most rightly have gained the whole world with a single drop of his most precious blood deems all the sorrow of his most worthy passion and death repaid by union with a single soul!

15. After this the Lord again intoned, *Rejoice, you righteous,*[19]* which all the host of heaven took up and concluded, as if wishing that soul joy. Then the Lord, in the person of the church still militant on earth, concluded by singing, "Refreshed with heavenly food and drink, we your suppliants beseech you, our God, that we

*see Ps 32:1

---

18. Antiphon for the feast of Saint Agnes, but replacing feminine with masculine forms (*juncta* with *junctus*, *quam* with *quem* and *posita* with *positus*).

19. Antiphon for various feasts, including All Saints and Common of several martyrs.

may be strengthened by the prayers of the one in whose memory we have received these gifts. Through our Lord Jesus Christ."[20] After this the Lord sweetly greeted all the saints and sang, "The Lord be with you," and at those words their glory, joy, and rewards in heaven were doubled in honor of that union that he had so courteously accomplished in that soul. Then, in place of "Go in peace," in the praise and glory of the shining and ever-tranquil Trinity, all the choirs of angels and saints made re-echo with a loud voice, "To you be praise and honor, Lord." Then the Son of God, stretching out his royal hand, blessed that soul, saying, "I bless you, daughter of eternal light, with such effect that from now onwards anyone for whom you have desired great things with special affection will be blessed before others, as much as Jacob, before his other brothers, once received good fortune from the blessing of Isaac his father." And at this, coming to herself, she was aware of her beloved held close by an indissoluble union in her inmost being.

To Jesus Christ our Lord be praise, honor, thanksgiving, and power, for ever and ever. Amen.

20. Postcommunion for the feast of Saint Agnes.

THE BOOK OF SPECIAL GRACE

PART SIX

Mechtild of Hackeborn

CHAPTER ONE

THE LIFE AND DEATH
OF THE VENERABLE
LADY ABBESS GERTRUD

Lady Gertrud, our abbess of sweetest memory, glorious and truly brilliant light of our church, who blossomed like a rose in all the virtues, exemplar of complete sanctity and a most solid pillar of true religion, was sister in the flesh of this blessed virgin of whom we have written.[1] From her earliest years she was wonderfully wise and discreet, so that they consecrated her abbess in her nineteenth year. She conducted herself so laudably, gently, and prudently in this office that she was held in great reverence and loved by all with the love bestowed on a mother, showing herself both to God and to men and women as lovable and full of grace.

The extent of her humility shone forth in her manner, gestures, words, and all her actions. She often joined the sisters for the lowliest of tasks and especially their common labor; she was sometimes the first, or even the only one, to set to work, until she persuaded her subordinates, or rather attracted them, by her example or her gentle words to help her. She was a lover of true poverty and for that reason desired that she and her subordinates should eschew all excess of worldly possessions.

1. That is, Mechtild of Hackeborn.

She took very great care of the sick, so that she was never too busy to visit each one every day and ask them sollicitously if there was anything they wanted, also serving them with her own hands, both for their rest and for their refreshment. Consequently, although she was burdened by innumerable infirmities in old age, she had herself carried to see the other sick women, and when she could not speak, she showed them such sincere compassion by gesture and nods that she moved very many to tears.

She was very accessible, and she loved everyone with such a motherly love that each one thought she was her favorite. As a result one could hardly tell which were her relatives in the flesh. Her character was so very sweet and gentle that when she had severely rebuked one of the sisters for a fault with good reason, she would immediately speak to her at the same time and in the same place as lovingly and softly as if she had never offended. She acted in the same way when she had made a serious accusation that justice required against someone in chapter: as soon as chapter was over, that sister would have safe access[2] to her. No sister was so young that she feared to disclose her problems to her with confidence. We never saw or heard her show herself harsh towards anyone without good reason, or cause them distress for a character flaw. In her own sickness she was so gentle and kindly, and so cheerful and patient in everything, that she made happy and glad all those who came to serve her.

---

2. See *Securum accessum jam habet homo ad Deum, ubi mediatorem causae suae Filium habet ante Patrem, et ante Filium matrem* (Arnold of Bonneval, *De laudibus beatae Mariae virginis* [PL 189:1726]).

Whenever she could, she used to read Holy Scripture with great care and wonderful delight, demanding that her subordinates should love the reading of Scripture and constantly recall it to mind. Consequently she used to purchase for her church all the good books that she could, or she had them copied by the sisters. She was also assiduous in encouraging the young girls to become proficient in the liberal arts, saying that since they would not fully understand Holy Scripture if the pursuit of learning were lost, the practice of the religious life would perish at the same time. And so she often compelled the younger, less educated girls to learn more, and she provided them with schoolmistresses.

She was most devoutly and intently constant in prayer, so that she rarely prayed without weeping. Her mind was completely untroubled, and at the time of prayer her heart was so free from cares that many times when she had been called from prayer to the window, or to other business, as soon as she returned she found once again the same purity of devotion that she had had in her prayer. Eventually she had carried her zeal for prayer and devotion so far that when in old age her strength and, to a certain extent, her faculties had failed and she had lost the use of speech, she would receive communion with the greatest reverence of devotion and with floods of tears, just as she had been accustomed to do all the days of her life.

And when the sisters talked to her about God, she showed with the greatest joy by her expression and by nods, as if giving thanks, how gladly she heard them; she was never so unwell that she did not become livelier, as if there were nothing wrong with her, when she heard talk, or just a word, about God. She wanted to be taken to Mass frequently, and she was astonishingly conscientious and devout concerning the canonical Hours, so much so that although she was drowsy in her sickness, or sometimes had food in her mouth or a cup at her lips to drink from, at the time of the Hours she always forced herself to be astonishingly alert.

She had also possessed from infancy a heart of the utmost purity, so that she would not listen to the slightest word that could produce a stain in her heart. What more can we say? All virtue, knowledge, and true religion were reflected in her as in a mirror. She was most fervent in charity and devotion with respect to God, supreme in loving-kindness and sollicitude with respect to her neighbor, foremost in humility and suffering with respect to herself. Among the children most sweet and gentle, among the younger nuns most holy and discreet, among the older ones most wise and joyful. She was never found idle; she was always either doing something useful with her hands or praying, or teaching, or reading. This is what she was like, and she ruled herself and those subject to her so laudably that, if I may say so, we have not seen her equal, nor shall we see her like again.[3]

After presiding over our monastery with great distinction for forty years, this woman began to be troubled with frequent infirmities. Since she had been sick for a year and more, and had in addition lost the power of speech, her loving sister, believing she was about to die, besought the Lord on her behalf as pressingly as she could that he would condescend to do with her according to the good pleasure of his will and the best interests of her soul. Suddenly her spirit was caught up

---

3. From *O virgo virginum, quomodo fiet istud? Quia nec primam similem visa es nec habere sequentem?* "O Virgin of virgins, how shall this be? For neither before you was any like you nor shall there be after," the eighth of the Advent O antiphons (referring to the Virgin Mary).

into heaven, where she saw in the mirror of the Divine Providence that she was not to die yet but would continue in that sickness for some time. Nonetheless, the whole host of saints was preparing with joyful haste for the arrival and welcome of so great a spouse of the Lord.

Among the other adornments with which the blessed Virgin Mary was wonderfully distinguished, she was holding snow-white gloves, on one of which appeared a golden eagle and on the other a golden lion. This indicated that that soul for whose reception she was preparing was like that glorious Virgin especially in three things: in virginal innocence, which was symbolized in the shining whiteness of the gloves; through exalted and far-sighted contemplation, which was signified by the eagle; and also through the constancy of the fortitude with which she defeated all vices, which was symbolized by the lion. In preparation for her the patriarchs and prophets were holding golden containers full of varied gifts, symbolizing that she had cared so wisely and faithfully for those subject to her in all things both physical and spiritual. The apostles, too, were holding massive decorated books before them, with which they were honoring her for the most wholesome teaching that she had provided for those subject to her, for by this she attained an apostle's reward. The martyrs were holding shining golden shields, with which they were to show the sick woman respect for her unwearying patience, by which she was valiantly protected against all adversities, and through which she had attained their reward. The confessors were made glorious with ample and most beautiful copes to show her respect for her monastic way of life and most holy examples, by which she attained their reward. But the virgins were holding golden crowns and shining mirrors in preparation for her, with which they were to soothe the sick woman for her innocence and purity, and because she was accustomed to examine her life very often in the mirror of the example of Jesus Christ, to see how far it was like, or unlike, God in virtues, and in this she was joined with, or rather set above, certain holy virgins.

CHAPTER TWO

THE SERVICE OF TWELVE ANGELS

After this, while her sister[1] was praying for her again, she saw her soul in the likeness of a transparent building, in the midst of which God was sitting and shining through it like sun through crystal. And the Lord said to her, "Just as there is nothing to stop you seeing me through this building, so you can know me in that woman's soul in all the virtuous deeds that she is practising right now, in particular, in patience, kindliness, and cheerfulness, which through God's grace are allotted to her supernaturally: all of these I perform in her and through her."

After this, she saw around the sick woman's bed twelve angels assigned to her service, who were reporting to the Lord everything that happened to her, both through her own virtues and also through those serving her. At her feet were three angels providing her with patience, which abounded in her so greatly that all twelve angels were needed to praise the Lord God for her. On her left were three archangels, who were serving her with respect to virtuous wills, intentions, and holy desires. On her right were three from the choir of thrones, who were providing her with tranquility, gentleness, and loving-kindness. At her head were three from the choir

---

1. That is, Mechtild.

of dominions, who received all the honor, reverence, and charity shown the sick woman by the sisters and bore it with joy to the sight of the highest King.

Then, since her sister was deeming it a sin that she was so glad to be with her, fearing lest perhaps she was yielding to human feeling more than she should, she asked the Lord about this. He replied to her, "This is not a sin for you; for almost all her senses and the impulses towards sin that she could have had have been removed, and I have led her to such a state that her life cannot displease in any way. Nowhere will you ever find me more truly and surely than in her and with her, except in the sacrament of the altar, and in her you will discover virtues most like mine. For just as I showed myself so kindly, gentle, and lovable to my disciples and to all men and women, so does she to those subject to her and to all those who now come to her. And just as I bore sweetly, cheerfully, and patiently all the pains and injuries inflicted on me, so she is enduring her sickness and sorrows with a sweet and joyful heart. And just as, out of my immense generosity, I distributed all that I had to those who crucified me, so she has now given away all that was hers."

CHAPTER THREE

THAT CHRIST STOOD PROXY
FOR HER

Another time when about to communicate, her sister was praying the Lord that he would condescend to stand proxy[1] for <the abbess>, and render due praise and thanksgiving to God the Father, because she could not speak for herself. The Lord replied, "I should do this, shouldn't I? For a robber would do this, who would either restore what he had taken or substitute something else for it if he wanted to make restitution. So I, who have deprived her of speech, shall certainly do this: because she cannot do it herself, I shall myself render it [i.e. praise and thanksgiving] a hundredfold."

It seemed to her as if the Lord were standing on the right of the sick woman, wearing a garment of purest gold, covered with bright green flowers. Embracing her most sweetly, he kissed her, saying, "To you, my spouse, I pledge a thousand thousand kisses." The Lord's golden cloak signified the love of his divine heart, and the flowers the green growth of all the virtues in which he flourished and exerted himself on earth. On his breast he had a most beautiful rose, also green in color, wonderfully adorned with precious stones, with which the sick woman was playing: this symbolized her trust in

---

1. That is, like a godparent.

God, which she had always in all things. Her face, too, shone with indescribable beauty, so that it seemed to <Mechtild> that she had never seen such grace in a soul. Her eyebrows were especially regular and fleetingly arched: this seemed to her to indicate her foresight, by which she used to arrange all that pertained to her office so far-sightedly. Her eyes shone with a remarkable light, signifying the gaze of her merciful kindness, with which she had regarded the neediness of those subject to her with great compassion and merciful kindness. Her mouth was rosy, indicating the persistence of her teaching and the abundance of her profitable words, with which she had been eager to instruct those subject to her and many others who came from a distance.

Again, when on one occasion her sister had received communion, she said to the Lord, "I beseech you, Lord, be mindful with what faithful zeal your servant demanded, sometimes with blandishments, sometimes with rebukes, that the sisters should receive communion frequently and gladly, and that now, hindered by sickness, she is not able to receive your worshipful Body, and condescend to bestow yourself on her, as befits your royal generosity." The Lord replied, "I have given myself to her as bridegroom and most faithful friend and sole consolation." She said, "How can it be true that you are her sole consolation, since she seems to take some delight in worldly things, accepting people's kindnesses and gifts with cheerfulness and a certain joy?" The Lord replied, "Should you not also consider that when you misunderstand her nods and act against her wishes, she smiles so kindly, just as if you had done her a great favor? And so you should know that she is firmly fixed in me in such a way that she behaves the same with respect to everything that happens to her, whether joyful or sad."

Again, another time when she was about to communicate, her sister saw the Lord Jesus as if he were a
young boy of twelve years old, extremely beautiful and
refined, embracing her with his right hand and, among
many other things, saying these words: "In return for
your right hand that I have taken from you, I shall be
your co-worker in all that you do; in return for your foot
and your leg, I shall be your guide. I shall adorn you
with perpetual virginity, I shall give you joy and happiness in return for all your infirmities. You will have eternal freedom of movement in return for every physical
burden; you will enjoy me with continual delight."

CHAPTER FOUR

HER HAPPY PASSING

After this, therefore, since that sunbeam was moving towards the sunset of death, and that dazzling crown of our glory was declining towards its end so that the Lord might make it more completely fit for himself, in a miraculous way he deprived her of the power of speech for twenty-two weeks, so much so that she could not indicate her requirements except by these two words, that is, "My spirit," with which she miraculously requested all that she needed. Thence it often happened that, misunderstanding her, they did not do what she wanted. However, she bore this with the greatest kindness and patience. For God, who directed all that happened to her by his sweetest spirit according to his most supreme pleasure, was indeed dwelling in her and with her. But since she used to repeat those words, "My spirit," so continually, on one occasion this sister of hers asked her, "And who is your spirit? Of which order of angels?" Immediately, speaking without difficulty, she replied, "My spirit is the seraph."

Nearly a month after her loss of speech, she was so unwell one morning that she was thought to be dying. And while the community was summoned and she was being hurriedly anointed, the Lord Jesus appeared to very many people dressed in beautiful form, as Bernard says,[1] stretching out his arms as if to embrace her and looking at her tenderly, and, wherever she turned, placing himself opposite the sick woman's face, as if he were anticipating her death with strong desire.

1. See above, p. 15, n. 5.

CHAPTER FIVE

THE SAME SUBJECT CONTINUED

And so that day arrived, for which she had longed with so many joyful desires and had secured with so many devout prayers, on which she began her death-agony; the Lord was seen to come quickly, all blithe,[1] accompanied on his right and on his left by his most blessed mother and the beloved disciple, John the Evangelist. After them followed a multitude from the whole court of heaven, and specially the armies of virgins, which seemed to fill that house during that day. They seemed to mingle with the community, which also remained there throughout the whole day, bewailing their desolation with tears and sighs and commending with devout prayers the passing of their mother. The Lord Jesus seemed to caress the sick woman with such exceedingly sweet gestures, which could worthily assuage the bitterness of death. And when the words *And bowing his head he gave up the ghost**   *John 19:30 were read in the passion, as if from excess of love the Lord Jesus leaned over the dying woman, opened his own heart with both hands, and stretched it over her.

1. See above, p. 16, n. 7.

CHAPTER SIX

THE HOUR OF HER MOST
HAPPY PASSING

And so that most happy hour was at hand at which
that heavenly bridegroom, the imperial Son of the highest Father, determined to receive his beloved, emerging
from the prison of the world, as she had long desired,
to rest with him in the wedding-chamber of love. That
happy soul, a hundredfold blessed, flew up with inestimable jubilation of delight to that uniquely excellent
tabernacle, that is, the sweetest heart of Jesus, opened
up to her so faithfully and joyfully. What human being
could guess what there she saw, what heard, what sensed,
what inhaled[1] with blessed love from the overflow of
loving-kindness—she who deserved to use so wonderful
a steed by special privilege?[2] Human weakness cannot
haltingly describe with what honey-sweet caresses in the
sweetest depths of her being the vigorous bridegroom
conducted her, and with what joyful dance those companions welcomed her with joyous crowns, at the very
moment that the glorification of so happy a soul was
accomplished with the festive praises of all! It therefore
befits us, together with the citizens of heaven, to sing a

1. See above, p. 19, n. 10.
2. See above, p. 19, n. 11.

song of jubilation with thanksgiving to God, the creator of all.

Therefore since that dazzling sun, which used to scatter its rays far and wide in our world, had set, and with respect to the Godhead that tiny drop had found once again the depths from which it had flowed, her daughters were left alone in darkness. Lifting up eyes of faith to the glory of their mother's blessedness through the aperture of hope, then did they truly pour forth tears from their heart. With loud voices they uttered praises to heaven, amidst heavenly gladness from joy in their mother's glory, and they entrusted their loneliness to her motherly affections with the response, "Arise, virgin."[3] In this, while they were chanting, "you who rest in the shadow of your beloved," she was heard to respond, saying, "It is not enough for me to be in his shadow, but I am reposing most sweetly and safely, or rather peacefully, in the heart of my beloved."

After this, when this virgin of Christ was earnestly praying one day, she saw the soul of her dead sister in shining glory, and blessed Benedict, the father of the Order, going on ahead holding a staff in his hand, and with his arm lovingly and respectfully embracing the happy soul of his daughter, that is, the same abbess, and leading her before the throne of the worshipful Trinity, and chanting with high voice to the honor and praise of that soul with most beautiful melody the response, *Who is this who goes forth like the sun?*[4] and so on. And when she had reached the throne, leaning gently towards her, the Lord said, "Welcome, my most lovely daughter." Then she sincerely prayed the Lord on be-

3. See above, p. 20, n. 14.
4. *Quae est ista quae processit sicut sol?* response for the feast of the Assumption.

half of the community for all that had been entrusted to her. Then she who saw these things [i.e., Mechtild] said to her, "What instructions do you wish to give your daughters, dearest sister?" She replied, "Tell them that they should continually love their most loving beloved with all the inner strength of my heart and soul, and they should by no means place anything before the love, or even the mindfulness, of him." Then <Mechtild> said, "Commend us all to God, for I see that all is well with you." To this she replied, "I commend my daughters to that most delightful rest in which I am living most securely: that is, the sweetest heart of Jesus Christ the most loving."

CHAPTER SEVEN

THE GREETINGS GIVEN
THAT MOST BLESSED SOUL

Then the handmaid of Christ saw herself in a dream, greeting the soul of her dead sister with these words: "I greet you, Christ's bride, in that love in which you burned when you first gazed upon the beautiful countenance of God your creator, its glory unveiled. I greet you, Christ's virgin, in the sweetness that you felt when you fully recognized, by experiencing it, God's inestimable love that he had felt for you from eternity. I greet you in the perfect beauty in which you shone when you received a most complete reward for all your deeds from the hand of the Lord, your king and spouse." When she had done this, she began to wonder how she dared to greet an uncanonized soul in such a way. And when, hesitating inwardly, she questioned the Lord on this, he courteously replied, "What you did was right and proper, for she is the glory of my omnipotence, the beauty of my wisdom, and the choice of my divine goodness."

A second time she saw her soul wonderfully glorious in a choir, with most lovely locks of hair that adorned her with wondrous beauty. Her elegant and vigorous spouse, the Lord Jesus, holding her hand, said, "Her virtues are more numerous than the hairs on her head."

Another time when she saw her in glory once again, she asked what kind of reward she had received for her practice of repeating so devoutly the psalm *Praise*

*Ps 116   *the Lord, all you nations,* * especially on the feast of the Resurrection. <The abbess> displayed to her bright green garments of wonderful splendor, in which she was dressed, and they were decorated with countless golden stars, and there were wonderfully varied embroideries, intermingled with white pearls and tiny red gems. Then <Mechtild> said to her, "Since you abound in all good things, what would you now like to give the sister who served you so faithfully in your sickness?" Touching one of the red gems, she said, "Take her this, from me." When she said, "Since I am seeing this in spirit, you well know that I cannot physically present her with this," she replied, "That white that you can see in the stitches of my garments signifies the humanity of Jesus Christ, which is sweetest above all grace, and the red of the tiny jewels signifies the passion of the spotless Lamb. So tell her that she should trust in God's mercy, for by my prayers I will obtain from my Lord that he should grant her clemency and that she should willingly accept hardships for his sake."

CHAPTER SEVEN A[1]

ON HER SISTER'S SOUL, AND THAT THE SOULS OF THE BLESSED OFFER TO GOD ALL THE WORDS RECITED FOR THEM

Another time, while the community was receiving communion, she saw the soul of her sister standing on God's right hand in inconceivable beauty, and the Lord was impressing on her as many sweet kisses as the number of people communicating. This represented the special reward that she had because she so conscientiously required the sisters to communicate frequently and willingly. While she was wondering at this and rejoicing in it, she also longed to know if the priest gained some reward for administering the sacrament of the Lord's Body to those who approached. The Lord replied, "Just as a knight would be made rich if he were carrying the king's only son to all the princes in his arms, and each one of them offered the king's son a hundred marks, and the king gave it all to the knight when he came back with his son, so the priest's reward is increased when

---

1. Corresponds to *Special Grace* 5.2. Although it is present at this point in the two manuscripts, Paquelin does not print this or the following chapter here because they had already appeared in *Special Grace* 5.

he administers the sacrament of the Body of Christ to the faithful with devout thanksgiving."

After this she said to her sister, "Tell me, dearest sister, what good does it do you when we recite the antiphons and responses of the Holy Trinity,[2] or some other prayer?" She replied, "I accept each and every word from your mouths like roses that I offer to my beloved with joy." And she showed her on her cloak most beautiful roses with a golden leaf in the center, and said, "This golden leaf is the leaf of the heart, that is, of charity, from which proceeds the power of prayer, for you all offer me such things out of charity, not duty." Then she said, "What happens to those offerings that we make to the saints?" She replied, "Each and every one accepts what is offered in the same way with thanksgiving, and they present it to God their King with joy; even if you recite just one Our Father for all the saints, with the intention that if you could you would recite one for each of them individually, at that moment they all receive it individually in its entirety, as if you had said it for each of them, one by one."

2. *Historiam sanctae Trinitatis.*

CHAPTER SEVEN B[1]

HER SISTER'S SOUL <AGAIN>, AND THAT HUMAN DESIRE LIVES ON AFTER DEATH

Again, when Mass for the dead was being chanted one day in the chapel in which <the abbess> had been buried, and <Mechtild> was reciting a series of antiphons and responses of the Holy Trinity in thanksgiving to God for the soul of her sister, the Lord said to her, "Would you like to see her now once more?" Immediately she saw her soul in great glory, with a truly splendid white veil on her head. She asked the soul what the veil symbolized. She replied, "It signifies my habitual disposition, and the godhead irradiates every one of this veil's threads with remarkable glory and splendor." From these words she perceived that anything performed by someone from customary devout habit, no matter how small, like something that supports veils and crowns, is not forgotten in God's eyes, and for it the soul receives special honor. And she asked, "Where is your crown?" She replied, "My crown is of such inestimable glory that it is raised up from earth to the throne of God and reaches the four corners of the world. It has its origin on earth because I have bequeathed my memory and my example to those on earth, but it is

---

1. Corresponds to *Special Grace* 5.1, paragraph 2–end.

lifted up to the throne of God because from my virtues God has thanks and honor and all the saints have joy. And it embraces the four corners of the world because my life has benefited the whole church and will do so until the end of time."

When she asked the soul about a certain matter for which she had prayed the Lord while she was still alive, she replied, "My prayer now has a more powerful effect, and brings about more profitable and fruitful things than at that time when I was on earth." When she asked her in astonishment how this could be, she replied, "It is so, for the prayer of the righteous, even while they are dying, by no means dies with them, nor does it fail, but the prayer and the desire of anyone who prays while alive for sinners, that they should not perish, will also be powerful after death. And so it is in other cases."

There is something similar to this in the second book of Maccabees, where we read that Onias, who *had been the high priest,** and Jeremias the prophet had appeared to Judas Machabeus, and Onias had said of Jeremias, *This is he that prays much for the people** and so on, although there is no doubt that the soul of Jeremias was in limbo. But he who when alive had pleased God as God's true priest with his prayers for the people is said to have prayed for the people even after his death. From this we can glean that if anyone extended their desire to the furthest reaches of the world, so that if possible they would be willing to go on living, and to benefit with their prayers, their desires, their labors, and their own suffering all those on earth and in purgatory for God's love and honor, without a doubt God would accept the will for the deed.

*2 Macc 15:12

*2 Macc 15:14

CHAPTER EIGHT

A VISION OF HER
ON HER MONTH'S MIND

On her month's mind, her soul again appeared to
<Mechtild> in new and surpassingly excellent glory,
flanked by glorious companies of heavenly princes, who
were all holding cymbals in their hands and, redoubling
the sweet sound of both the cymbals and their voices, were
chanting this verse, *Praise the Lord on high-sounding
cymbals,* * and so on. And when that most blessed soul   *Ps 150:5
was conducted amid such chants to stand before the throne
of the King of Glory, Jesus, her sweetest lover, addressed
her as follows: "You are welcome, my dearest." In this she
perceived a most sweet accomplishment of the Godhead:
how by its absolute omnipotence, just as it loves every
single person in that love, so it directs its attention as if it
loved no one except that one person. Thence breaking out
from the abundance of overflowing sweetness in praise
of her lover and spouse, she chanted, *My soul melted.*[1]*   *Song 5:6
After this, rewarding his beloved for the excellence
of her praise, the cantor of all cantors, who is the beginning and end of every perfection, intoned the antiphon
as if from out of himself, the abyss of complete blessedness. With sweetest voice he chanted, "O Gertrud,
O pious one!" Following this with delightful sound,

---

1. Antiphon for the feast of the Assumption.

the whole court of heaven added, "How pious is it to
rejoice in you, O Gertrud, equal of prophets!" In these
words <Mechtild> understood that she was especially
praised because she was so trusting on earth and had
great delight in all God's gifts. And she was praised
for the spiritual instruction that she had delivered to
those subject to her with these words: "Associate of the
apostles, jewel of prelates, by faith and merits distinguished in piety, mercy, indescribable love: ever exult,
here and before God!"[2]

Then her sister, who saw these things, said to her,
"Tell me, I beseech you, dearest sister, what is that
melting of which you sang, 'My soul melted'?" She replied, "When the most unrestrained love of the Godhead
floods and penetrates a soul in such sweet power that it
is impossible for a created being to absorb it completely,
then she [i.e. the soul] flows back, inwardly melted and
dissolved, into that very source from which she received
the largesse of such great blessedness." Then her sister
said, "Pray for your daughters, who embraced you on
earth with such faithful love." To this she replied, "I
have done so, and I do so unceasingly." And her sister
said, "What commands do you wish to give them?"
She said, "That the sweetness of the love that remains
in my inmost heart may also remain in their hearts and
minds." Then her sister added, "What were you given
when you first arrived in heaven?" She replied, "The

2. Adapted from *O Martine, O pie, quam pium est gaudere de
te, O Martine, prophetis compar, apostolis consertus, praesulum
gemma, fide et meritis egregius pietate, misericordia, caritate
ineffabili; succurre nobis nunc et ante deum,* "O Martin, O pious
one, how pious it is to rejoice in you, O Martin, equal of prophets,
associate of apostles, jewel of prelates, by faith and merits distinguished in piety, mercy, and indescribable love: help us before
God!" Antiphon for the feast of Saint Martin of Tours.

Lord God, my creator, redeemer, and lover, received me, filled me with inestimable joyfulness, and dressed me in himself, fed me with himself, and giving himself to me as bridegroom, glorified me with indescribable honor."

CHAPTER NINE

THE ANNIVERSARY OF
THE SAME LADY ABBESS

On the anniversary of this lady abbess of sweetest
memory, when the response "My redeemer lives"[1] was
being chanted at its Vigils, her sister saw her soul embracing the Lord Jesu with inestimable joy and delight,
and chanting the same words most sweetly; by divine inspiration she knew that the souls in heaven rejoice with
inestimable joy in Christ's humanity, and as often as
people on earth chant these words intently, or anything
else concerning their future resurrection, they make it
re-echo at once with unspeakable joy, seeing that very
truth in Christ's glorified humanity. Convinced that they
too will rise again, they pray for those who sing these
psalms on earth, that they too should deserve worthily to
attain that blessedness. She also knew that when people
devoutly offer these words, their own bodies are sanctified through faith as a result, so that they may enjoy
this glory more worthily.

After this once again she saw as it were God the
Father sitting at the royal table with that soul, caressing
her with sweetest and most loving words and gestures,
as if his only joy and delight was to feast with this soul
in this way. The Lord Jesus, like an imperial youth,

---

1. Response for Vigils for the Dead.

girded with a towel, served at that table varied dishes
sweetened by the Holy Spirit. One by one the members
of the community, coming in procession, knelt with
great reverence and offered caskets of ebony, silver,
and gold, filled with a wonderful scent. Those women
who excelled in purity of heart were carrying ebony
caskets, and those who labored in God's service more
than others had silver ones, but those who surpassed
others in fervor of love were carrying golden caskets.
In addition, a multitude of souls, arriving with joy, were
offering great thanks for their own release to God and
to <the abbess's> soul, to whom God had given them
to glorify her feast. Then all the souls of their community, both the brothers and the sisters, were circling
around her like dancers. Among them she saw the soul
of a brother who had died in that same year in a pure
white stole, adorned from above with wonderful and
varied beauty; she understood that this symbolized his
kindliness, for he had had a very kind heart, showing
good will in everything.[2] Those leading the dances were
singing most joyfully, "O our mother"[3] and so on. And
out of the heart of the Lord Jesus came a great trum-
pet into which passed the sound of all the voices with
sweetest modulation.

   The next day, when Mass was being celebrated for
the same soul, this desire came to <Mechtild's> mind,
that if she were an all-powerful queen, she would like to
offer God at the altar a golden statue, most excellently
robed and adorned, for her sister's soul. Immediately the

---

2. This must be the soul of Brother Seguinus: see LDP V.11.
   3. *O mater nostra, ter sancta quaterque beata, cum prece
devota famulantum suscipe vota*, "O our mother, thrice holy and
four times blessed, receive your servants' offerings with devout
prayer"; response for the feast of Saint Catherine of Alexandria.

Lord responded to her thought: "What if I were to fulfill this desire of yours myself?"And straightway the Lord appeared, standing before her in the form of a royal, or rather divine, youth, shining in splendor, and said, "Look! Take me, and offer me according to your every desire." With unspeakable desire and thanksgiving she embraced him and took him with her to the altar. The Lord Jesus offered himself to God the Father with all his virtues for the increase of that soul's perfect beauty, and with the joy, sweetness, and love of his divine heart for its eternal joy and blessedness.

After this that most happy soul, as if she had become her spouse's powerful queen, rushing most lovingly into God's embrace, led him around through the choir to each of the sisters, saying to each, "Welcome the Lord of virtues, and ask him for virtues." Then she who saw these things said to her, "My dearest sister, what service do you most wish us to offer?" She replied, "Humble obedience, loving charity towards each other, and faithful attention to God in all things." And she added, "Ah, give your heart wholly to love, and love all people; then the love of God and of all those who have ever loved God will be wholly yours. Similarly, if you are humble, the humility of Christ and of all those who have humbled themselves for his name's sake will truly be yours. And if you show mercy to your neighbor, the mercy of God and of his saints will also be yours, and know that it is the same with all the virtues."

Therefore may God be blessed in his gifts, and holy in all his deeds. Amen.

THE BOOK OF SPECIAL GRACE

PART SEVEN

Mechtild of Hackeborn

CHAPTER ONE

THE LAST DAYS OF THE
BLESSED SISTER MECHTILD,
GLORIOUS VIRGIN, NUN AT HELFTA

This humble and devout handmaid of our Lord Jesus Christ, loving mother and sweet comforter of us all, the subject of this book, had reached in praiseworthy fashion the fifty-seventh year of her life in religion and was at the peak of all virtues. Having been vexed for nearly three years by continual suffering, she began to draw near her death.

For on the second-last Sunday [i.e. of the liturgical year], that is, If <you, O Lord, will mark> iniquities,[1]* God's chosen one received the life-giving sacrament of the Body and Blood of Jesus Christ for the last time before her death. A person devoutly attentive to God saw the Lord Jesus standing before the sick woman in inestimable glory and saying with refined countenance and gesture, "My divine nature's honor and joy, my human nature's crown and reward, my spirit's delight and repose: do you wish to come and abide with me more fully, to fulfill your desire and mine?" To this she replied, "My Lord God, I desire your praise more than my own health and salvation. Therefore I ask that I may still make recompense in my sufferings for all that ever

*Ps 129:3

---

1. See above, p. 39, n. 3.

a creature neglected in your praise." Most graciously accepting this answer, the Lord said, "Because you have made this choice, you will become like me in this, for I voluntarily undertook the sufferings of the cross and death for the glory of God the Father and the salvation of the world. And just as all that I endured pierced the divine heart of my Father, so your sufferings and death will penetrate my heart to its inmost depths, and they will profit the whole world for its salvation."

CHAPTER TWO

HER SUMMONING BY THE LORD
JESUS CHRIST

Again, another woman heard that the Lord summoned her with these words, "Come, my chosen, my dove, my flowery meadow where I found all that I desired; my lovely garden, where I enjoyed every delight of my divine heart; where there were flowers of every kind of virtue, trees of good works,[1] and waters of devout and fervent tears: she was always open to whatsoever I wished. Whenever sinners irked me, I took my rest in this garden, and drinking from its water I became drunk, so that I no longer remembered all the injuries done me."

---

1. See LDP II.3.1, lines 15–17.

CHAPTER THREE

SHE IS DIVINELY WARNED
TO BE ANOINTED

Then, a person,[1] devoutly praying, was warned in spirit by the Lord, so that for her part she could warn <Mechtild> to prepare to receive the sacrament of the anointing of the sick. He asserted that for her own part she was to tell her that after the reception of that life-giving sacrament he, the most attentive Guardian of his friends, would himself protect her most carefully in his bosom from every spot, just as a painter guards the picture he has just painted with the greatest care, lest it should be obscured by dust. (It was also revealed to another person that the Lord wished her to be fortified by the sacrament of holy anointing on that very day.)

<Gertrud> told the sick woman this but did not want to do anything to forward matters herself, as she was always subject to her superiors in all things, humbly submitting to their decree. Instead she completely entrusted herself to Divine Providence, who has never abandoned those whose hope is in him. But her superiors held her in such great regard that they had no doubt she would certainly know in advance the time that it would please the Lord for <Mechtild> to receive this sacrament, so when they saw that she was not insisting

---

1. Gertrud again: see LDP V.4.4, lines 3–10.

or urging this, they put off the sacrament of anointing on that day. But the Lord, validating that verse from the gospel, *Heaven and earth shall pass, but my words shall not pass,* *demonstrated the truth of the word that he had spoken to his chosen one by this proof: before Matins on the Monday, blessed M\<echtild\> of happy memory began to be so afflicted by sudden pains that she was most certainly thought to be dying. Priests were then hastily summoned, she received the sacrament of the anointing of the sick, and so it happened that she was anointed, although not on that very day,[2] nonetheless before dawn on the next day.

2. That is, the Sunday.

CHAPTER FOUR

EACH OF THE SAINTS GAVE HER ALL THE FRUITFULNESS OF THEIR REWARDS WHEN SHE WAS BEING ANOINTED

It was revealed to three persons that the Lord was most courteously present in the form of an elegant spouse and was himself offering the life-giving sacrament to his chosen. Among these people, it seemed to one[1] that while the sick woman's eyes were being anointed by the priest, with a ray of divine splendor the most loving Lord turned towards her most graciously the full gaze of his divine loving-kindness, which constantly moves his heart, flowing with honey, in its own goodness. With that splendor he gave her the use of his own most holy eyes. Then she saw <Mechtild's> eyes exude, as it were, a liquid of sweetest oil out of the abundance of the divine loving-kindness. She perceived from this that through her merits the Lord was generously condescending to bestow the succor of consolation on all those invoking her with confidence. And she earned this privilege because she always showed herself kind and well-disposed towards everyone, with loving charity.

1. Gertrud: see LDP V.4.5.

In the same way, when the other limbs[2] were being anointed, at each one the Lord granted her most perfect use of his own most holy limbs. But at the anointing of her mouth,[3] uncontrollably zealous for her soul, he most graciously prepared to offer his spouse a kiss on the mouth, surpassing a draught of honey;[4] with this he bestowed on her all the fruitfulness of his most holy mouth.

When they were reciting in the Litany, "All you holy seraphim and cherubim, pray for her," <Gertrud> saw that, with the deepest reverence and greatest dance of exultation, those blessed seraphim and cherubim moving away from one another had offered God's chosen one a most suitable seat among themselves and spiritual understanding from the very fount of all wisdom, and with the fiery seraphim had embraced the one who is *a consuming fire.** She therefore should be placed among them on high, as they deserved above all others to be near the divine majesty.

They considered that on earth she had led the life of an angel through the holiness of her virginity, and, even more than the angels, with the cherubim she had drunk copiously streams of spiritual understanding from the very fount of all wisdom, and with the fiery seraphim she had embraced the one who is *a consuming fire.** She therefore should be placed among them on high, as they deserved above all others to be near the divine majesty. And when the saints were named in the Litany, each of them rose up with immense joy and the greatest reverence, and kneeling presented their merits to the Lord's bosom in the form of precious gifts, to increase the joy and glory of his beloved. When the anointing was

*Deut 4:24

*Deut 4:24

2. In the Middle Ages, seven parts of the body were anointed.
3. See above, p. 40, n. 5.
4. See above, p. 41, n. 7.

finished, the Lord embraced her most lovingly and supported her for two days so that the wound of his sweetest heart lay open at the sick woman's mouth. Every breath that she drew, she seemed to breathe in from there, and to breathe out again into the sweetest heart.

CHAPTER FIVE

HER DEVOUT INTENTION
AND HER HUGE
AND FERVENT DESIRE FOR ALL

Therefore the most joyful time of her blessed passing was approaching, at which after the weariness of
various sicknesses, the Lord had determined to give
his chosen one the uninterrupted sleep of eternal rest.
On the Tuesday, that is, the vigil of the feast of Saint
Elizabeth,[1] it was obvious before None that she was beginning her death agony. The community had gathered
with great devotion and, in expectation of the death of
their sister in Christ, so dear to them, with the greatest
sorrow were fortifying her with the customary prayers.
One of them,[2] led by more burning desire, saw her
soul in the form of a most delicate young girl standing
before the Lord and breathing out every breath that she
breathed in through the wound in the most holy side,
into that heart that was flowing with honey. As a result,
as often as the deified heart, moved by the unrestraint
of its own kindness and sweetness, drew in her breath, it
overflowed from superabundance of love and sprinkled
showers of grace throughout the breadth of the church,
and specially on those there present. She perceived that

1. See above, p. 42, n. 8.
2. Gertrud: see LDP V.4.7, line 9.

this was because at that moment, thanks to God's gift, that blessed woman in her sickness had a specially devout intention and fervent desire for all those, both living and dead, to whom the Lord generously dispensed his gifts of grace.

CHAPTER SIX

THAT THE BLESSED VIRGIN MARY ACCEPTED FROM HER THE CARE OF THE COMMUNITY, ENTRUSTED INTO HER HANDS

While they were reciting the antiphon "Hail, queen," at that phrase, "Ah, therefore, our advocate," the sick woman, God's chosen one, lovingly addressed the Virgin Mother and commended to her the sisters whom she was close to leaving. She prayed that she would receive them to greater love for her sake. Just as she had offered herself while alive to them all, as far as she could, as a benevolent and willing advocate, so the Mother of Mercy herself would now, after her death, condescend to be perpetual mediator and advocate of the community with her before her Son. The spotless Virgin showed herself most willing to do this and, stretching out her delicate hands to the hands of the sick woman, accepted the care of the community entrusted to her as if from her hand.

CHAPTER SEVEN[1]

THE PRAYERS RECITED
BY THE SISTERS AT
THE SICK WOMAN'S BED

Then while they were reciting the prayer, "Hail, Jesu Christ," at this phrase, "sweet way," the Lord Jesus, tender spouse of her soul, appeared, as if smoothing the way for his bride with the oil[2] of his divine nature, that he might draw her to him more sweetly and tenderly. [When the community had repeated their prayers before the sick woman until after the hour of None, and the sick woman had begun to improve somewhat, she was asked whether the community could go to dinner. The sick woman replied, "They can certainly go."]

And in this way she lay dying all day, and said nothing except, "O good Jesu! O good Jesu!" showing most openly that deep in her heart was fixed the one whose name, in the midst of the bitter pains of death that her physical gestures made clear, she constantly ruminated so sweetly in her mouth. And when the sisters one by

---

1. This chapter is not in the Wolfenbüttel manuscript. Paquelin retranslated it from the old German version and pointed out that much of it occurs in LDP V.4 (specifically, LDP V.4.8, lines 13–17, 4.9, 4.10, and 4.11). Here the passages in square brackets are those not found in LDP and therefore solely dependent on the German.

2. See above, p. 43, n. 9.

one devoutly entrusted themselves to her prayers and commended to her whatever their needs and preoccupations might be, she would at least murmur "Gladly," or "Yes," even though she could not say any more. She expressly declared by this the love with which she was commending to the Lord her lover whatever had been entrusted to her. [Finally, when she could no longer speak, she was nonetheless unable to control the goodness of her sweet love, with which she loved her fellow sisters and spiritual friends; for again and again she raised her eyes above her to heaven and stretched out her hands lovingly. Through this she made plain her love for God on behalf of those who had been entrusted to her.]

The person mentioned earlier [i.e. Gertrud] perceived that from all the limbs of this blessed sick woman in which she was tormented there issued, as it were, an extraordinary exhalation that, as it passed through her soul, purified her miraculously, sanctified her, and made her fit for eternal blessedness.

Although this person had seen all this in spirit, she decided inwardly that she would keep all these things secret, lest she should be made conspicuous in this. But what followed made clear that this was contrary to the Lord's goodness, *whose glory is to search the speech** and who said, *That which you hear in the ear, preach upon the housetops.*†

For during Vespers it once again seemed to be so obvious that this chosen one of God, Lady M<echtild> of happy memory, who was very sick, was dying that the community was quickly summoned from choir, so much so that they had to omit the suffrages, and were repeating the customary prayers over the sick woman. But however strongly she exerted her inner senses, the woman mentioned earlier could not even perceive or note the least thing of what the Lord was doing at that

*Bernard, SC 65.2, and see Prov 25:2

†Matt 3:27

time concerning the sick woman until, examining herself, she acknowledged her guilt and, washing it away through sorrow and repentance, promised the Lord that she would willingly make known whatever he deigned to reveal to her, to his glory alone and for the consolation of her neighbors.

Then after Compline, while for the third time they were quite convinced that the sick woman was about to die, the person mentioned earlier was caught up in spirit, and she saw the sick woman's soul, as before, in the form of a very tender and lovable little girl, but as it were made lovely with new adornments from that day's sufferings, rushing impetuously to the neck of Jesus Christ, her delicate spouse, and holding him with heartfelt embraces. Like a bee sucking all kinds of flowers, she drew to herself a special pleasure from each of the Lord's wounds.

When they were reciting the responsory "Hail, spouse"[3] and so on, the Queen of virgins, Mary, rose without a thorn, the worshipful Mother of God, came forward and rendered the soul of the sick woman more and more fit to enjoy and take pleasure in divine delights. Then from the merit of his untouched mother and from that dignity by which she alone deserved the grace of being mother and virgin, the Lord Jesus took a necklace, as it were, made of wonderfully glittering gems and placed it on the sick woman's breast, at the same time endowing her with the special privilege that she too should be called mother and virgin, like his own Virgin Mother, considering that she had given birth in chaste love to mindfulness of him in the hearts of many.

3. See above, p. 44, n. 10.

CHAPTER EIGHT

CHRIST GREETS THAT BLESSED SOUL IN AN INCONCEIVABLE WAY

And so on the night of the feast of Saint Elizabeth, when Matins had already started, God's chosen one again showed such changes that it was thought that she was now breathing her last. So abandoning Matins, the community quickly gathered around her in the customary way. Then, shining in the splendor of his divine strength, the Lord appeared dressed like a bridegroom, *crowned with glory and honor** and miraculously adorned by the beauty of his indescribably dazzling divine nature. Addressing the sick woman's soul with sweetest caress, he said, "Soon, my beloved, I *shall exalt you among your neighbors,** that is, in the presence of the community so dear to me." And thus in a way beyond understanding or thought, and far exceeding all human comprehension and unheard in any age, he greeted that most blessed soul in a new manner of greeting, through each of the wounds of his most holy body, which are said to number 5490, so that each wound emitted four wonderful manners [i.e. of greeting], that is, of most delightful sound, of most potent exhalation, of most abundant dew, and of most lovely splendor. Through these the Lord continuously greeted his chosen one and summoned her.

And so the sweet sound, which surpassed every kind of musical instrument, symbolized all the words that

*see Ps 8:6

*Sir 15:4

God's chosen one had spoken, together and individually, throughout her life for the salvation of her neighbors, either sweetly to God, or profitably for God. For all these, made sweet and multiplied a hundredfold in the divine heart, she was rewarded by the emissions of each of the Lord's wounds. The truly wonderful exhalation symbolized all the desires that she had had for God's praise, or for God's sake, for the salvation of all. These too were repaid her, multiplied by a power beyond human understanding, through each of Jesus' sweet-flowing wounds. The generous dew expressed every feeling of love that she had ever felt for God, or for another creature for God's sake, which also affected her soul with indescribably sweet-flowing delight through the Lord's wounds. The dazzling splendor symbolized the various physical and spiritual sufferings that she had endured from childhood until the present, which having been ennobled beyond all human capacity in union with the sufferings of Jesus, sanctified her soul and made her fit for divine brightness.

Resting in the enjoyment of heavenly delights, that soul did not expire at that moment but aspired to the loftier good things to be made ready for her by her lover. Copiously sprinkling those present with the generous dew of his divine blessing, the Lord said, "Touched by my own goodness, I was inwardly delighting in the sweetness of love, that all the members of this community, so dear to me, should be present at this transfiguration of my most worthy <beloved>. From this they will have honor in heaven in the presence of all my saints, as great as those three, chosen above all, that is Peter, James, and John, have above the other apostles, because they were worthy to be present at my transfiguration on the mountain." Then she asked, "Lord, what good can your generous blessing and copious infusion of graces do those who do not taste this inwardly?" The Lord replied, "When someone is given a fruitful orchard by his lord, he cannot taste each fruit at once, but he must wait until the fruit ripens. In the same way when I grant someone gifts of grace, they do not immediately experience the taste of inner pleasure until through the practise of exterior virtues, having completely shattered the outer shell of earthly pleasures, they deserve to relish the kernel of inner delight." Then having received a most salutary blessing from the Lord, the community once again re-entered the choir and finished Matins.

CHAPTER NINE

THE HOLY TRINITY AND
THE SAINTS GREET HER SOUL

Now when they were chanting the twelfth response,
"O lamp"[1] and so on, the sick woman's soul appeared,
standing in the sight of the supreme Trinity, devoutly
praying for the church. Sweetly chanting the same
words, God the Father greeted her, saying, "Hail, my
chosen one, for through the example of your holy life
you can rightly be called *lamp of the church, you who
pour out rivers*, that is, *floods of oil*, that is, of prayers,
throughout the length and breadth of the world." Then
God the Son intoned sweetly, "Rejoice, my spouse, you
who are rightly called medicine of grace, for by your
holy prayers grace is restored more abundantly to the
various people who lack it." Then the Holy Spirit sang,
"Hail, my spotless one, you who will deservedly be
called nourishment of faith, for in all hearts that piously believe in my divine work that I am working in
you, spiritually and not physically, the virtue of faith is
nourished and strengthened."

Then God the Father granted her from his omnipotence that she might provide protection to all those
trembling from human weakness and not yet fully confident in the divine goodness. Also the Holy Spirit, who

1. See above, p. 47, n. 11.

is called a consuming fire, bestowed on her that out of the fervor of his own divine love she might offer warmth to the lukewarm. Then the Son of God granted her, in union with his most holy passion and death, that she might bestow *healing* on all those *languishing* in sin. Then a multitude of holy angels, honorably lifting her up before the Lord, made resound together with clear voice, "You are the abundance of God, a fruitful olive, whose purity illuminates, and whose works shine forth."[2] In that phrase "whose purity illuminates," in consort they especially praised in her the most delightful repose with which the Lord worthily reposed in her soul. In that phrase *her works shine forth*, <they praised> the most praiseworthy and most single-minded intention of all her works. After this, all the saints sang the antiphon "God openly revealing to all <peoples>" and so on.[3]

2. See above, p. 48, n. 12.
3. See above, p. 48, n. 13.

CHAPTER TEN

DRAWING HER WITH HIS BREATH, IN A WONDERFUL WAY JESUS CHRIST MAKES THAT SOUL FIT FOR FUTURE GLORY

During the preface at High Mass, as if endued with a new and glorious splendor, Jesus, the vigorous bridegroom, gently seizing his bride's chin with his elegant hands, once again turned his spouse's face with sweetest caress so directly opposite his own face that he seemed to draw in the sick woman's breath directly by the breathing of his divinity. Placing his own deified eyes opposite her eyes, he wonderfully gazed upon her, and, faithfully sanctifying her, in a way he as it were made her blessed, and thus he fitted her for the glory of future blessedness.

During this, that woman who knew these things in spirit[1] perceived that she was not to be taken up until, all her strength almost completely exhausted and annihilated by the divine power, she would deserve to be made one in spirit with him, like a drop of water in a jar of wine, stripped of all human insipidity and plunged into the very abyss of all blessedness. And so, although the community had already offered the customary prayers five times for her, nonetheless she did not take flight.

---

1. That is, Gertrud.

Now after Terce, stretching out her legs of her own accord, that sick woman composed her feet like her crucified Lord, that is, putting the right foot over the left. And when the foot that she had put on top was replaced beside the other by the bystanders, she firmly drew it back and, once more putting it on the left foot, clearly demonstrated that she had not done this accidentally but with devout love, so that, conformed in body to the likeness of her one and only lover, she might at the same time deserve to be fashioned according to his glory. And in this way, repaying as far as she could the Lord, whose hands and feet for her love were fixed to the cross at the hour of Sext, voluntarily stretching out her legs during the time of Sext <Gertrud> offered a sacrifice to his eternal praise. Then she saw the Lord, as a dearest friend, touching her sick and dying limbs with sweetest caress.

CHAPTER ELEVEN

HER FLIGHT AND HER WELCOME
WITHIN THE DIVINE HEART

Then that most desirable hour was at hand when
that tender spouse of Christ Jesus, now purged of all
that is human and perfectly prepared according to the
most excellent pleasure of her beloved, coming out of
the prison of the flesh, was about to enter the marriage
chamber of the imperial bridegroom. The convent rose
up from their meal, and while the abbess of the monastery, with certain others, was standing by her, the sick
woman's face, suddenly transformed to most charming sweetness, displayed most certain power of inner
pleasure, as if inviting her dear sisters in Christ, whose
arrival she could not welcome with words but did so
nonetheless with a smile and a friendly expression, to
wish her well for the indescribable blessings bestowed
on her by the Lord.

Then the Lord of majesty, *flowing with delights,** *Song 8:5
the only satisfaction that satisfies the soul that loves
him, encircling her completely with the light of his divine nature, completely illuminated her. The Singer of
all singers was intoning most sweetly, and with music
surpassing all human capacity, *Come, you blessed of my
Father, possess the kingdom** and so on, reminding her   *Matt 25:34
of that most worthy gift by which for eight years[1] he

1. See above, p. 49, n. 15.

233

had given her his divine heart with the same words as a pledge of love and security. Then, greeting her most caressingly, he said, "And where is my present?" At this with both hands she opened her own heart directly opposite the heart of her beloved, and the Lord pressed his own most holy heart to hers and blessedly united her in her entirety, absorbed by the power of his divine nature, to his glory. There may she, mindful of those mindful of her, obtain for us a continual shower of rain by her holy prayers from the superabundance of her delights from him with whom, having become one spirit, she will exult for ever!

CHAPTER TWELVE

THE SAINTS' JOY AND
THE INCREASE OF THEIR MERIT

After this, when the commendation of the dead was being recited in the customary way, the Lord appeared seated in the majesty of his glory, gently caressing the dead woman's soul as she rested in his bosom. When they were reciting "Come to her assistance, you saints of God; run to help her before the Lord, sustain her soul,"[1] the angels, rising up with great reverence, as they had no need to sustain one whom they saw being welcomed with such great condescension by their Lord and honored so magnificently, knelt before the Lord, like princes accepting estates from the emperor, and received back their own merits, which they had offered the day before to increase the merit of Christ's beloved, as if they had been doubled by her merits and miraculously ennobled. Each of the saints did the same when their names were invoked in the Litany.

Then she who saw these things reminded the soul that she should pray for the failings of her special friends, with that affection with which she had loved them in this life. She replied, "I now see clearly in the light of truth that all the affection that I felt on earth for someone is scarcely, as it were, a single drop compared

1. See above, p. 49, n. 16.

to the vast expanse of that ocean of sweetest love felt towards them by the divine heart. I also see by how incomprehensibly useful a dispensation the Lord allows some failings to persist in a person, by which they are humbled and often distressed, and thus day by day he promotes their salvation. For even with the least thought I could not will anything other than what my sweetest and most loving Lord's all-powerful wisdom and most wise benevolence has decreed for each of these according to his good pleasure. So I exert myself completely in praise and thanksgiving for the disposition, so well ordered, of the divine loving-kindness."

CHAPTER THIRTEEN

HOW TO PRAY TO GOD THROUGH THE MERITS OF THIS VIRGIN

The next day, during Mass, that is, "Rest eternal,"[1] this woman's soul appeared, putting forth golden pipes from the heart of God for all those who had a special devotion to or love for her; through these pipes they could draw whatever they desired from the divine heart. Each pipe had a golden stopper,[2] which they had to extract to obtain whatever they desired by saying these words, trusting that through such words they could more easily attract the divine benevolence for whatsoever they desired:

A PRAYER THAT SHOULD BE FREQUENTLY RECITED FOR GOD'S GIFTS IN THIS VIRGIN

Through the love by which you ever blessed your beloved Mechtild or any of your chosen, or would have done had you found the potential in them, and will still do so in heaven or on earth, hear me, most kindly Lord Jesus Christ, through her merits and those of all your chosen.

---

1. See above, p. 50, n. 17.
2. See above, p. 51, n. 18.

Indeed, at the elevation of the Host, that blessed soul seemed to desire to be offered to God the Father together with the Host, to his eternal praise for the salvation of the whole world. Then God's Only-Begotten, who is not accustomed to deny the desire of his beloved, drew her in completely and, offering her to God the Father with himself, most courteously from that union granted double salvation to all his chosen in heaven and on earth and in purgatory.

CHAPTER FOURTEEN

THE UTILITY OF OFFERING CHRIST'S MERITS AND THOSE OF THE SAINTS FOR SOULS AT THE OFFERTORY

Also, during the subsequent Mass she appeared as if resting in the divine heart, playing four most beautiful chords on that heart, flowing with honey, like a sweet-sounding organistrum, making resound a most alluring descant of praise, thanksgiving, pleading, and prayer; that is, they were chanting a recompense sufficient for the negligence of all those who were present celebrating her funeral rites, and also for all those in the whole world who would gladly celebrate them if they knew all the blessings freely bestowed on her by God. Then at the offertory she was asked what came from this, that at the offertory she offered the merits of Jesus Christ and the saints for souls. Bending, she seemed to distribute caskets full of boxes, offering them to souls situated in various places of suffering. Each of them received a box with great delight, and as soon as they opened it, they were snatched up from all their sufferings and established in a most beautiful resting-place.

The caskets that she offered the souls symbolized her own virtues: the boxes the practice of virtues, such as humility, goodness, compassion, and the like, that she herself practised through her actions. Thence when she aimed particular caskets at particular places of suffering, the souls staying there who possessed any of that virtue on earth were transferred from suffering to joy. And in this way, to the increase of the joy and glory of his chosen one, the Lord transported countless multitudes of souls to the threshold of heaven. And as for those who justice demanded were not yet ready to enjoy heaven, nonetheless for the love of his lover, he allowed them to enjoy delightful places of blessed peace.

CHAPTER FIFTEEN

NO CHRISTIAN SOUL ENTERED HELL ON THE DAY OF HER PASSING

The same revelation concerning the release of souls[1] was divinely granted to two other[2] people. But one also knew in God that the following was true: that on that day when her happy soul passed away, from the overflow of the kindness of Christ's sweetest heart, not one Christian soul in the whole world descended into hell. For all the evil-doers who died on that day either arrived at <a state of> penitence by the merits of a soul so happy and so beloved to God, or if they were so completely wicked and hardened that they had deprived themselves of all grace, the Lord did not allow them to leave the body on that day lest such a harsh judgment should rage against any soul on the day of his heart's joyful and great solemnity.

1. That is, chapter 14.
2. That is, other than Gertrud.

CHAPTER SIXTEEN

GOD'S PRAISE SHOULD BE SOUGHT ABOVE ALL THINGS AND RENDERED WITH SINGLE-MINDED INTENTION

Again, in one of the Masses she appeared resting gently in the Lord's embrace; when she who saw these things tried to speak to her, the Lord opened his arms and quickly sent the soul away. Then she saw the soul surrounded with unspeakable glory, wearing a bright garment as if made from crystals; some were shining like stars, some bright like mirrors. They were all surrounded with golden circles, and through each a jewel lit up the crystal. Some of the jewels were red, some purple. Some were green; others showed various colors and types <of gems>. This garment was silken underneath and had been made from the good deeds and the virtues of that happy soul. The crystals symbolized her works; the golden circles showed that she had done all her works in charity, the gems the virtues of Christ that she had added to her own, for she did all her works in attentive union with Christ's virtues. And when she rose up she spread out that garment, as if inspecting it and seeing herself in it; it was very full and of such great splendor that it lit up the whole of heaven with new glory. And it gave out a tinkling sound of such great sweetness that its resonance moved heaven and all that was in it.

Then she who saw these things asked her what particularly she wanted from her own community. She replied, "I desire above all my Lord's praise, for he has glorified and exalted me so much more than I deserve that all he has conferred on me he seems to have given me from his generous loving-kindness alone. And so I find it most welcome that <all of> you should praise him unceasingly on my behalf. He has himself placed me at last among those saints in whom he takes the greatest pleasure, and in whom he delights most excellently and is most greatly praised." She said, "And how should we praise the Lord together with you?" She replied, "All that you do, I was doing when I was on earth. Therefore, briefly, whatever you do, do in union with the single-minded intention and perfect love in which I did all things to God's praise and the profit of the whole world. For instance, when you come into choir to praise or sing, think how single-mindedly and ardently I was intent on God and, as far as you can, take pains to imitate me. Similarly, when you go to sleep or to eat, think with what single-minded intention and ardent love I accepted the needs of my body and the use of created things. And so on in other things. In this way, let all that you do result in praise of my lover, and it will result in salvation for you yourselves." Then <Gertrud> said once more, "And what do you gain from our praising God on your behalf?" She replied, "A unique embrace and a kiss, in which every joy of mine is renewed." Then she saw three rays from God's heart stretch out to all the saints through <Mechtild's> soul; wondrously illuminated and made joyful by them, they began to praise the Lord through that soul, saying, "We praise you for the lovely beauty of your bride, for your loving pleasure in her, for the perfect union by which she is made one with you." And when <Gertrud> saw the Lord taking great delight in this praise of him, she said to him, "My Lord, why do you take such great pleasure in being praised in this soul?" He replied, "Because in her life she always desired my praise above all, and so she has retained that desire that she had, and I long to satisfy her with my unceasing praise."

CHAPTER SEVENTEEN

THE NAME OF THIS BOOK, THAT IS, "OF SPECIAL GRACE," AND ITS UTILITY

Then once again she asked that soul what glory she had received for her singular gift of grace. She replied, "This surpasses all my glory. For the most unrestrained love that made God become human freely infused this gift into me by his powerful wisdom and divine sweetness and most generous kindliness." When she asked if it was dear to her or troublesome that a book had been written about these things, the soul said, "It is a source of greatest joy, for I know that praise of my God, good will, and profit for my neighbors will result from it. For that book will be called the light of the church, for those who read it will be enlightened by the light of knowledge and from it will recognize whose is its inspiration, and the sorrowful will find consolation in it." Therefore anyone who loves this gift, it truly belongs to them as to the one who received it from God, just as someone who receives a royal gift from a messenger possesses it as their own and gains as much profit from it as one who receives it from the king's hand. For in this gift God alone wishes to have praise, glory, and thanksgiving.

CHAPTER EIGHTEEN

AN ASSURANCE FOR THOSE CELEBRATING HER FUNERAL RITES

Then when at the burial the response "Free me, Lord" was being chanted, she appeared intently praying the Lord for all those there present and celebrating her funeral rites, that they should never experience eternal death. On this she was deemed worthy to receive in promises from the generosity of the divine kindliness a definite assurance. Also when the response "the kingdom of the world"[1] was being chanted, at those words, "whom I have seen," she was singing, "Truly I have seen him in his divine nature, whom I glimpsed with the eyes of my understanding so often on earth, 'whom I have loved' with all my strength, 'in whom I have believed' with my whole heart, whom I have adored with all my affections."

And turning to the convent she said, "I ask you all and enjoin you to chant and recite this response gladly, for in it we make God the Father joyful, we greet the Son of God, we delight the Holy Spirit. And so you should think that the Lord would have entrusted this to Sister Mechtild to recite, except that he rejoices inestimably to hear it recited by you." Thence when the response, "Arise, virgin," was also being chanted to her, she

1. See above, p. 25, n. 17.

appeared standing before the Lord, like a queen most suitably adorned, and rushing into the Lord's embrace she leaned her head against his heart. The Lord said to her, "Joy and delight of my heart, all that is mine is yours; according to your wish, I will stand by and hear in their hour of need all those standing by who have taken part in your funeral rites."

CHAPTER NINETEEN

OUR LORD JESUS CHRIST LOVES HIS OWN AND CHASTISES THEM

After this, on the feast of Saint Catherine[1] she appeared with God, passing through the choir and conducting the singers in her usual way. When she who saw this marveled at it, the soul replied, "When I sang with you in choir with all my heart and all my strength, when the chant was ascending I carried you and your desires upwards, to God and into God, but when the chant was descending I brought grace from God back to you again with all my affections, and I am still doing this without pause." Then <Gertrud> said, "What instructions do you want to give the sisters?" She replied, "Rejoice heartily in your beloved, whose love for you is most tender and loving, like a mother's for her only child: from her extraordinary affection she always wants him to sit on her lap, so that she can protect him from all dangerous paths. And so God your lover desires that you should cling to him and never take a different path; when you do not do this, he allows you to suffer until he calls you back once more, like a conscientious mother who corrects her child with blows when he leaves her and falls over, so that through this he may learn not to go far away from her. And just as the mother is pleased that

1. November 25.

her child caresses her with loving words, so even more
generously does your lovable spouse desire to hear your
words, so much so that they penetrate the depths of his
divine heart. Ah, give him your whole heart, for he is
your father, your lord, your spouse, your friend, and he
is all in all to you." Divinely inspired, she understood
this to mean: because he is our father, we should entrust
every good thing to him; because he is our spouse, we
should love him with all our heart and soul; because
he is our friend, we should trustingly show him all our
troubles and needs and be comforted by him alone.

CHAPTER TWENTY

THE BLESSED SOUL OF COUNT B<URCHARD> OUR FOUNDER

Then within the month after her death, on the anniversary of Count B<urchard>, founder of our monastery,[1] she saw the count's soul in wonderful splendor, wearing a purple tunic adorned with all the virtues, and over it a white garment made up of red and green. On the red part were lions surrounded with golden circles, from whose hearts there seemed to come out most beautiful roses; on the part colored green all the virtues shone out with indescribable workmanship. He had a collar, too, like splendid stars, and a cloak of red gold, of the utmost purity, of clear silver underneath, and on his head an extremely beautiful crown. Then she who saw these things said to him, "Whence do you have such copious variety of such great virtues?" The soul replied, "I did not earn this magnificent grace by my own merits, but I enjoy it from my God's loving-kindness and the virtues of the community that I love. As for this tunic, decorated with all the virtues, I received it at the ascension of a magnificent queen, that is, Lady Gertrud the abbess. For she entered the celestial palace in distinguished glory, with numerous virtues and riches, like a powerful queen,

---

1. He died on the feast of Saint Lucy, December 13, 1229.

*see
1 Kgs 10:2

so that that verse in Kings, *The queen entered into Jerusalem,** could be said of her.

"For a long time, no soul like hers or as great as hers, with such magnificent virtues and such varied adornments, has entered the halls of heaven. Similarly I have this red and green garment from the merits of that abbess: it is made up from the virtues of those subject to her. The red color signifies the glory of martyrdom, which religious obtain by true obedience. For anyone who has voluntarily offered their own will to God sacrifices a more worthy and more precious victim than the head of their body. The lions express strong works of obedience; the circles, the bonds of obedience; the roses, the patience that religious ought to have in all their works. The green color expresses the verdant vigor of all the virtues, and then the wonderful decoration below represents clearly the reward of each virtue, and I possess this splendor from the merits of every single person who serves the Lord in my monastery. This collar designates the excellent desire of that abbess because it looks like stars, for just as a star is very pure, so was her continuing desire, for she always desired God's praise above all, and the salvation of her neighbors. The gold and the jewels that adorn this collar indicate her heart's zealous toil that she had from desire. But from her merits the Lord gave me this golden cloak, which signifies love and knowledge, and this crown of love: they were acquired not long ago, when that wonderful eagle[2] sought the secrets of heaven."

Then she said, "Ah, teach me what joys the saints had on that occasion." The soul replied, "When she had received communion for the last time in her sickness, she

2. That is, the abbess Gertrud.

was so closely united to God that we saw her enclosed in
God in heaven, and a new ray coming out of the Godhead
lit up all the saints, in which we saw and recognized
every reward and diginity that that most happy soul was
about to receive. And consequently we were making
ourselves ready in great and festive joy. At her passing,
the Lord drew in her soul with his divine breath with
such great sweetness and gentleness that it cannot be
expressed. Also, all we saints were there, from the greatest to the least. And when the Lord caught her up, all
the saints at once, rejoicing most sweetly, were singing,
'Prudent and watchful virgin, how happy are you with
that spouse who has chosen you!'[3] At those words, 'How
lovely you are, how wonderful, shining with so great a
light!'[4] that soul, abounding in delights, like a bride from
the wedding chamber, came forth from the divine heart
and stood before the throne, clothed in the Godhead and
completely filled with God. Then when the saints sang,
'Rejoice in the royal wedding chamber, you who are
united with God's Son,'[5] the Lord again embraced her
most lovingly and sweetly chanted in her praise, 'She
is lovely among the daughters of Jerusalem as you have
seen her, filled with love and affection' for God and
neighbor,[6] 'in the beds,' that is, in contemplation, 'and
in the scented gardens,' that is, in fruitful teaching, with
which she labored in the hearts of her neighbors.

"All the saints offered her merits to God, in honor of
her spouse; when I approached among them, the Lord,
embracing me most sweetly, gave me this gold cloak,
which is a symbol of love and knowledge, from the

3. Antiphon for the feast of Saint Catherine of Alexandria.
4. Antiphon as above.
5. Antiphon as above.
6. Antiphon for the Common of Virgins.

merits of his beloved, and placed a crown of love on my head. From then onwards I possessed greater knowledge and love for the Trinity, ever to be worshiped, and I will do so for ever." Then she said, "What does this splendor that surrounds you <all> signify?" The soul replied, "In this light I recognize God's goodness and mercy towards me, and I experience his ineffable love and sweetness, with which he has loved me from eternity." Then, when she asked him what good it did him that his anniversary was celebrated on earth by the community with festive chants, he replied, "My Lord dispatches all that is done for me to purgatory for souls, and as a result very many are released, and he gives me these souls as my own, just like an emperor who grants knights to his princes: and this will be perpetual honor to me in heaven."

CHAPTER TWENTY-ONE

GOD'S EXTRAORDINARY LOVE
FOR THE SOUL OF
BLESSED SISTER MECHTILD

During the month after her death, when <Gertrud> once again saw the soul of M<echtild> of blessed memory and questioned her about her glorious state, she replied, "As for my reward and my glory, *eye has not seen, nor ear heard, nor has it entered into the human heart.*"* Hearing this, she began to be sorrowful, but the soul comforted her, saying, "Dearest sister, do not grieve, for when a child longs to embrace his father but is unable to reach up to his father because he is small, out of great love and compassion the father bends down to the child so that he can kiss him and embrace him. In the same way the kindly Lord graciously bends down to the loving soul and shows her the unseen and unspoken secrets of heaven through comparisons. But I have been borne in triumph into the Godhead and most blessedly united with it, so that I have in some way become all powerful from the all-powerful, wise from wisdom, and kindly from kindliness, and am thus endowed with all the good things that are in God. And so the Lord has accepted in its entirety all that you lavished on me during this past month in prayers and in thanksgiving for me and in other good works, as if you had all done them for him, and he has heard your prayers according to the good pleasure of his most kindly will. In addition,

*1 Cor 2:9

whatever you requested with pious devotion and faith
at the tomb of my dear sister, know that you have been
heard, except that if what you requested is not expedient
for you, God's most merciful generosity will change
it for something else that is better and more useful for
you." Then <Gertrud> said, "Do all the souls of the chosen possess that most happy union with God of which
you have spoken?" The soul replied, "Yes indeed, but
it varies according to their desert: some surpass others
in nobility, others in knowledge, and so it is with all
of them."

CHAPTER TWENTY-TWO

THIS SOUL TO SOME EXTENT COMPARED TO THE BLESSED VIRGIN MARY IN HER VIRTUES

During Mass, when the glorious Virgin Mary appeared to her, she asked her if this happy soul was in any way like her. The kindly Virgin Mary replied, "Yes indeed: she seems very like me in all virtues, but in seven in particular. That is, particularly in humility, for she considered herself as nothing and did not set herself above anyone, and for this the Lord has set her among the loftiest saints. Second, in cleanness and purity of heart and innocence of life, for which she is now associated with those who are closest to God and especially abound in knowledge of him. Third, in faithful love, for which every good thing that the soul is able to receive flows into her more potently: that is, joy, delight, honor, and blessedness. Fourth, in desire for God's praise, which led her to seek God's praise on earth and promote it in all that she could. And for that reason she has been set among those who praise God with the greatest pleasure, and the Lord counts all praise and thanksgiving performed for her as if it had been offered to him. In addition, he wishes to fulfill all her desires that have not been fulfilled. Fifth, in mercy and compassion, for which she received this honor: that she is able to assist all those who call upon her in their hour of need. Sixth, in kindliness and gratefulness; for that reason she is like a fountain into which God flows, in whose overflow all the saints are bathed in remarkable joy and bless the Lord for her. Seventh, in intimate union, because of which she is still associated the more intimately with God. In addition, she has earned this special prerogative, that God condescends to hear all those who have worshiped God through that mutual love with which God loved her and she loved God." And she added, "From that day on which God took away your mother whom you all loved as your own soul, he entrusted you to me in that faith and love with which he chose me as his own mother. Hence my every endeavor is how fittingly to adorn you as bride for my son. But now because he has deprived you of this your comforter, he has restored himself to you as comforter with all that he is."

SCRIPTURAL INDEX

References are indexed by chapter and paragraph in *The Herald of God's Loving-Kindness*, Book 5; by paragraph only in *The Mass Celebrated in Heaven*; and by part and chapter in *The Book of Special Grace*.

Exodus
16:33-34 Herald 1.9
19:14 Mass 9
31:18 Herald 1.9

Numbers
7:89 Herald 1.9
17:10 Herald 1.9

Deuteronomy
4:24 Herald 4.6;
Special Grace
7.4 (x2)

1 Kings
10:2 Special Grace
7.20

2 Kings
4:34 Herald 27.1

1 Chronicles
29:17 Mass 9

Nehemiah
8:10 Herald 17.2

Esther
1:11 Herald 1.5

Job
10:7 Herald 33.1

Psalms
2:7 Mass 1
8:6 Herald 4.12;
Special Grace
7.8
20:4 Herald 1.2
21:2 Herald 7.4
21:25 Herald 1.3
23:10 Herald 7.4
24:1 Herald 7.4
31:8 Herald 1.36
32:1 Mass 15
33:9 Herald 36.1
33:19 Herald 1.8
34:13 Herald 19.3
41:2 Herald 27.1
41:3 Herald 30.9
44:3 Herald 7.4;
9.3; 9.5;
30.1
44:5 Mass 7
44:11 Mass 7
49:14 Herald 1.16
50:3 Herald 5.6

54:23 Herald 36.1
68:17 Herald 5.6
70:18 Herald 10.1
77:30 Herald 1.4
105:45 Herald 11.1
116 Special Grace
6.7
129:3 Herald 4.4;
Special Grace
7.1
144:9 Herald 12.4
150:5 Special Grace
6.8

Proverbs
8:31 Herald 1.8;
Mass 6
25:2 Herald 4.10;
Special Grace
7.7

Song of Songs
1:3 Herald 7.5
1:13 Herald 30.2
2:10 Herald 4.18
2:14 Herald 23.2
2:16 Herald 2.1